THE
MAKING OF AMERICA
SERIES

HARNETT
COUNTY
A HISTORY

Seven Harnett fishermen enjoy a successful day on Cambro Pond. (Courtesy Dan Maynard.)

THE
MAKING OF AMERICA
SERIES

HARNETT COUNTY
A HISTORY

JOHN HAIRR

ARCADIA

Published by Arcadia Publishing,
an imprint of Tempus Publishing, Inc.
2 Cumberland Street
Charleston, SC 29401

Printed in Great Britain.

Library of Congress Catalog Card Number: 2002103800

For all general information contact Arcadia Publishing at:
Telephone 843-853-2070
Fax 843-853-0044
E-Mail sales@arcadiapublishing.com

For customer service and orders:
Toll-Free 1-888-313-2665

Visit us on the Internet at http://www.arcadiapublishing.com

CONTENTS

Acknowledgments   6

Introduction   7

1.   Natural History and Native Americans   9

2.   Colonial and Revolutionary Era   19

3.   The First Seventy Years of Independence   35

4.   Founding of Harnett   49

5.   War for Southern Independence   61

6.   The Lean Years   73

7.   Political Turmoil and Prosperity   89

8.   Roaring Twenties and the Great Depression   117

9.   The Modern Era   137

Bibliography   153

Index   157

ACKNOWLEDGMENTS

A work of this nature is impossible to complete without the assistance of many individuals who have shared their knowledge of Harnett County. I would like to acknowledge the gracious assistance of Lieutenant Colonel Sion Harrington III for his suggestions on the text. Steve Massengill of the North Carolina Department of Archives and History was a valuable resource in locating historical images of Harnett County.

To everyone down through the years who has shared an anecdote or story about Harnett's fascinating past, a hearty "thank you."

INTRODUCTION

In 1996, Kirsty Sutton of Arcadia Publishing contacted me about putting together a book telling the history of Harnett County, North Carolina through old photographs. The result of this effort was *Images of America: Harnett County*, released in 1998. This book, its pages filled with historical images and old maps, has been, I am grateful to say, well received by those interested in the history of Harnett.

The *Images of America: Harnett County* book served its purpose, but still, it had its shortcomings. Since the book was primarily a pictorial work, the content of the written part of the book was extremely limited, and it was virtually impossible to explain many of the incidents of the county's fascinating past in detail. On numerous occasions, individuals that have perused the *Images* book have encouraged me to write down the history of the county to accompany the visual presentation.

In the year 2001, Mark Berry, an editor with Arcadia, contacted me with details of a new series of historical books his company was putting together. This series, the *Making of America*, presents the history of locales across the country using written narratives as well as photographs. Seeing this as a wonderful opportunity to present the written history of the county, I accepted his offer to put together a volume about Harnett for this series.

The book you now hold in your hands, *Harnett County: A History*, is the result.

1. NATURAL HISTORY AND NATIVE AMERICANS

Harnett County consists of 595 square miles located near the very center of North Carolina. To the north lies the state capital, Raleigh; to the south lies the commercial hub of Fayetteville; while to the southwest is the world's largest military installation—Fort Bragg. All have influenced the county in one way or another throughout its history, yet Harnett has been able to maintain a distinct identity.

THE LAND

Harnett is geographically diverse, sitting astride the boundary between the Piedmont, Sandhills, and the Coastal Plain. Each portion displays characteristics of these different physiographic regions.

The northwestern portion of the county lies within the Piedmont and is characterized by swift creeks, red soils, and steep hills. The highest elevation in this section near Cokesbury reaches 470 feet above sea level. This is the only portion of Harnett from which iron and coal have been extracted.

The eastern margin of Harnett, along the boundary with Sampson and Johnston Counties, is a region of swamps and lowlands. Mingo Swamp, whose tannic-stained waters creep along the county's eastern border, is known for its cypress trees and water moccasins.

A region of rolling hills and fertile soils lies immediately west of these swamps. It is bounded on the west by the Cape Fear River from the Cumberland line up to Lillington, then west to Fish Creek and Hector's Creek, and on the east by the lands drained by Mingo Swamp.

Soils are productive here, having been farmed for more than 250 years with great success. In addition, all of the county's major commercial and manufacturing centers are located here, including the incorporated municipalities of Erwin, Dunn, Coats, Angier, and Lillington.

Just west of this section is a region known as the Flatwoods. This region derived its name from the fact that the relief of the land is generally level and was once covered by a vast pine forest. The Flatwoods cover the portion of the county south of Lillington to Linden, then up Little River to Elliott's Bridge, north to Flat Branch Church, thence back to Lillington.

The southwestern portion of the county lies within the Sandhills of North Carolina. This region is characterized by large sandy ridges that are often separated by swamp-filled valleys. At one time, these sandy hills were covered with longleaf pines, but the turpentine industry depleted the supply of these trees, so today the predominant vegetation is scrub oak, wiregrass, and slash pine.

Though an unnamed peak approximately 1,000 feet southeast of Mount Moriah Church off N.C. Route 27 is the highest point in the county at 490 feet above sea level, the most famous of these sandy hills in Harnett is Cameron's Hill. Located just east of Johnsonville, Cameron's Hill was long regarded as the highest point in Harnett, with some old accounts giving it an elevation greater than 650 feet. In actuality, it is only about 485 feet above sea level.

Until the last decade of the twentieth century, the Sandhills were the most sparsely settled section of Harnett County. This was due to the barrenness of the soil and the reliance of the inhabitants on the products of the forests for their sustenance. Small settlements grew up along the major transportation arteries: Spout Springs, Olivia, Pineview, and Mamers along the railroads, and Johnsonville along the Fayetteville and Western Plank Road.

This is a view of the Cape Fear River from the Duke Bridge in 1910. (Courtesy Coastal Piedmont Leader.*)*

NORTH CAROLINA RIVER BASINS

This map of the river basins of North Carolina shows the importance of waterways to Native Americans and early settlers.

CLIMATE AND WEATHER

The Southeast Regional Climate Data Center contains records of observations made at official weather stations across the southeastern United States. The only station within Harnett County is located on the Black River south of Dunn. According to this data, collected between 1962 and 1999, the average maximum temperature in summer is 87 degrees, while the average low temperature in winter is 31 degrees.

The average annual precipitation is 47.2 inches, over half of which usually falls between April and September.

It should be pointed out that the weather in Dunn is usually a few degrees warmer and the town normally receives more annual rainfall than do the northern and western portions of the county.

The hottest temperature ever recorded in Dunn was 108 degrees on August 22, 1983. The coldest day was -4 degrees on January 21, 1985. Bear in mind that these temperatures are for the 37 years of the end of the twentieth century, and it is likely that these extremes have been exceeded in times past before records were officially kept in the county.

11

Certainly the county has known cold conditions and harsh winters in the past. For example, it is known that the Cape Fear River froze over in 1893, 1899, and 1917.

The largest rainfall events recorded in Dunn each coincided with hurricanes. The largest one-day rainfall occurred on September 16, 1999, when 7.4 inches of rain fell during the bombardment of Hurricane Floyd. The second largest occurred during Hurricane Fran on September 6, 1996, when 6.5 inches fell. As with the temperature, it should be remembered that the official rainfall measurements were more than likely exceeded in times past when records were not officially maintained. The tremendous rains that fell on the area during at least three major events—Charlie Teigen's Hurricane in 1856, the Freshet of 1908, and the 1945 Freshet—produced floods in Harnett of much greater magnitude than anything experienced in the late twentieth century.

Harnett has also seen several large snowfalls. These would include notable snowstorms in 1856, 1899, 1927, and 2000. The most fierce of these likely occurred during the brutal winter of 1856, but the greatest twentieth century snowstorm occurred in March of 1927. The snowstorm of January 2000 is noteworthy for dropping nearly two feet of snow in some parts of the county.

WATER RESOURCES

Harnett County is a land of rivers. In fact, four different rivers flow across the county. In addition, there are numerous creeks, branches, and streams. The waters from all of these watercourses eventually enter the Cape Fear River and make their way to the Atlantic Ocean.

Black River rises in the northeast near the Wake County line north of Angier and flows south by southeast, separating the towns of Dunn and Erwin before crossing into Cumberland County. Beyond Rhodes Pond, Mingo Swamp flows into Black River, which thereafter becomes South Black River. The designation "South" was added by Sampsonians, who refer to another tributary as Black River. The folks in Cumberland and Sampson commonly refer to South Black River simply as South River, while Harnett residents cling to tradition and call the stream by its original name: Black River.

Upper Little River begins near Lemon Springs in Lee County at the junction of Little Juniper Creek and Mulatto Branch. A short distance downstream from the community of Carolina Trace, Upper Little River flows into western Harnett County. The river flows over several gravel shoals, and joins the Cape Fear River opposite Erwin. A set of rapids located just downstream of the N.C. Route 210 bridge south of Lillington was long known as "Great Falls of Upper Little River" and served as a mill site for nearly two centuries.

Lower Little River rises in western Moore County and flows east through the Sandhills of Moore, Cumberland, and Harnett to its junction with the Cape Fear near Linden. This watercourse is significant to the county as it forms much of Harnett's southern boundary with Cumberland County.

Lanier's Falls are on the Cape Fear River near Raven Rock.

This view from the Erwin Bridge shows the Freshet of October 1929.

The most important river in Harnett is the Cape Fear, which flows across the county dissecting it into two roughly equal halves. All of the creeks, branches, streams, swamps, and rivers of Harnett eventually join the Cape Fear and enter the ocean beyond Bald Head Island.

In the early days of settlement, the Cape Fear was the main transportation artery for people and goods. In the days before bridges were constructed, it was an obstacle to travel that divided the county and created an intense rivalry among the inhabitants of the respective sides. Since the middle of the twentieth century, the inhabitants have looked to the Cape Fear as their primary source of drinking water.

As it flows through Harnett, the Cape Fear drops nearly 85 feet and passes over the Fall Line, the rocky transition zone between the Coastal Plain and the Piedmont. Plunging across this line, several sets of rapids and falls are created. The most significant set of these are Smiley's Falls, a series of rapids near Erwin where the river drops 25 feet in 1.5 miles.

There are numerous springs scattered across Harnett. In the old days, the county's inhabitants often utilized these springs as a source of drinking water. Some of the more noteworthy springs include Gourd Springs near Anderson

Creek, Spout Springs in western Harnett, Chisolm Springs south of Johnsonville, Blacksmith Spring at Summerville, and the spring near the Spring Hill Methodist Church near Mamers.

One of the most widely known of these old springs is the Flora MacDonald Spring on Cameron's Hill, where the famed Scottish heroine gathered water while living nearby with her sister Annabella.

Legend maintains that Flora would sit on a rock by the spring, whiling away the hours waiting for her husband and son to return from their trip west in search of land on which to settle.

The most famous of all these springs in Harnett is Chalybeate Springs, located between Lillington and Fuquay-Varina. These mineral waters were known at least as early as the War for Southern Independence and became the focal point for a popular health resort in the early twentieth century. Though no longer a tourist attraction, the spring still flows, and a community in northern Harnett still carries the name.

MINERAL RESOURCES

Harnett County has never been known as a source of great mineral wealth like some of its neighboring counties to the west. But from time to time minerals have been extracted from the ground with some profitability.

Iron was once mined from the Buckhorn Hills in the northwestern portions of the county. The Buckhorn Mine, Douglas Mine, Pegram Mine, Battle Mine, McNeill Mine, and Dewar Mine all yielded the red rocks that were smelted into iron at the Buckhorn Furnace along the Cape Fear near the mouth of Parker's Creek.

Ore was extracted from these mines from the 1850s through the 1880s, and Harnett was an important source of iron for the Confederate arsenal at Fayetteville during the War for Southern Independence. According to former state geologist Jasper Stuckey, Harnett has the distinction of being the site of the first modern blast furnace erected within North Carolina to process iron.

Gravel has been an important mineral extracted from Harnett. Large-scale operations have extracted the rocks from the terraces along the Cape Fear and Upper Little Rivers since the 1920s when the gravel was first identified as being in such abundance that it would be commercially viable to extract it.

Kaolin is a mineral resource that was once important to many of the county's residents who consumed it for its purported healthful benefits. Though it is unclear whether it was ever dug on a commercial scale within the bounds of the county, individuals often visited sites where layers of this material had been exposed in road cuts or creek banks and dug quantities for personal consumption.

This may seem odd to hear of people eating dirt, but it should be noted that kaolin is the main ingredient of a popular medicine sold under the trade name Kaopectate.

In recent years, sand from the Sandhills has been extracted and sold in large quantities. Sand pits now dot western Harnett, exposing the clay base of many of the sandy hills.

One other very important mineral that was once reputed to have been extracted from the land now called Harnett was gold. In his report on the natural resources of his district for the 1850 Mortality Census, enumerator R.B. Smith of the Northern Division of Cumberland recorded the following note: "Gold has been discovered in many places in the Northern part of this District. No mines in operation." The exact location of these deposits, or the amounts taken from the ground, are unknown.

ABORIGINAL INHABITANTS

Except for a small band of Native Americans who resided in the Buckhorn area, no tribes were resident in what is now Harnett County when the first settlers arrived. But artifacts, burial mounds, and two important trails give mute testimony to the presence of Native Americans in the centuries before the first European settlers arrived.

This view of Mingo Swamp shows the dense foliage early settlers faced.

Campbell's Falls on the Cape Fear River near Erwin posed problems for early navigators.

In the days since the settlers first tilled the soils, inhabitants of what is now Harnett have turned up various arrowheads, spear points, and other artifacts from their Stone Age predecessors. This was especially true in the early portion of the twentieth century when many of the county's farmers began using tractors and heavy plows, thus tilling the earth deeper and exposing previously undisturbed layers of dirt.

More visible signs of the presence of the ancient inhabitants were the burial mounds scattered across the county. Little is known about the people who constructed these mounds, or why. They are all reported to have been used in part for burial purposes.

One mound that the early settlers came across was located at the mouth of Indian Branch, near where N.C. Route 210 crosses Upper Little River. Historian Malcolm Fowler once described this mound, stating that, "these particular graves were once a mound, roughly circular with a diameter of about forty feet and as high as a man's head. Cultivation over a period of 180 years has reduced the mound to a mere rise in the surrounding terrain."

The most well-known Indian Mound in Harnett was located in the western portion of the county near the Moore County line. The earliest extant description of this site appeared in a Fayetteville newspaper, the *North Carolinian*, in 1850. The correspondent noted, "The soil is sandy, and numerous holes are dug about in it, and a number of bones have been exhumed. A large number of beads have been dug in former years."

A more complete description of the mound was published in a newspaper from Southern Pines in 1909. Newton Zuver, a barber by trade in Southern Pines, obtained permission from John A. Cameron, who owned the land, to study the mound. In his report, Zuver noted, "Careful measurements showed the mound to be about fifty feet long, thirty feet wide and not far from twenty-five feet high. A few hour's work with the spade brought to light skulls, arms and various other bones of the human body. Of course, these bones had become separated and much decayed by the long lapse of time since their owners were fighting for their homes and hunting grounds."

Very little remained of the site by 1940 when Fowler accompanied a group of archaeologists from the University of North Carolina to the site. By the end of the twentieth century there were no visible remains of the mound except for a few bone fragments, though the mound is still prominently displayed on the U.S. Geological Survey's topographic quadrangles.

Two important transportation routes used by the aboriginal inhabitants are known to have crossed what is now Harnett County. One of these trails cut across the northwestern portion of the county and forded the Cape Fear at the mouth of Donnelly's Creek. This trail connected the Pee Dee area with southside Virginia.

Greens Path to the Pee Dee, an old trail that led from southern Virginia to the Grassy Island Ford on the Pee Dee River, entered Harnett County near Bailey's Crossroads and traveled south on the ridge separating Mingo Swamp and Black River. The trail crossed Black River at a ford near the present bridge at Baersville, and proceeded southwest to a ford across the Cape Fear near the mouth of Little River.

This trail was utilized by its namesake, Reverend Roger Green, during his travels and explorations in the area in the 1650s. It would also be utilized in coming years by settlers moving south out of Virginia into North Carolina.

2. COLONIAL AND REVOLUTIONARY ERA

The earliest documented event known to have transpired in what is now Harnett occurred in 1711, during the Tuscarora War. Colonel John Barnwell and his army, composed primarily of Native Americans from South Carolina, traveled north from their home province to aid the settlers of North Carolina against the Tuscaroras. When Barnwell's army reached the Cape Fear at the mouth of Lower Little River at the site of the ford across the river where Green's Path crossed, they were forced to construct log rafts on which to cross the rain-swollen river. At his campsite on the eastern side of the river, Barnwell took a quick count of his forces and found that many of the Native Americans had deserted. He was joined by a Captain McKay, who had been dispatched further upstream to recruit more natives for his army.

As the troubles with the Tuscaroras ended, settlers began penetrating into the interior of North Carolina. They came by different routes into the land that eventually became Harnett. Many came south out of Virginia, following Green's Path to the Pee Dee and taking up the first available lands that were not already claimed. Those who traveled this route were predominantly of English descent, sometimes the second generation born in the colonies.

Other settlers moving south out of Virginia utilized another Native American trail to get into the region. This trail cut across the northwestern portion of what is today Harnett and forded the Cape Fear at the Gist Ford, also known as Donnelly's Ford, at the mouth of Donnelly's Creek. Many of the people who eventually settled in northern Harnett came down this route.

The most important transportation arteries used by the early settlers to penetrate this area were the watery highways of the Cape Fear and its tributaries. Canoes, piraguas, and flat boats brought the majority of settlers and their belongings up these rivers to the interior of the province. For many years the river remained the transportation artery of choice for those who lived in the region. That is why the first land taken up by settlers was located along the Cape Fear and why so many of the settlers built their cabins facing the rivers.

No one knows for certain when the first settlers arrived in what is now Harnett County. The area was far removed from the center of Colonial authority in the early eighteenth century. In addition, North and South Carolina both claimed the land on the west side of the Cape Fear River, which would have made the area unattractive to those who wished to secure a title or a grant to land.

The remoteness of the area was attractive to those seeking to avoid government interference in their affairs or to escape the long arm of the law. There is a persistent legend that Harnett's first settlers belonged to the latter category, as they are reputed to have been pirates who fled up the Cape Fear in 1719 when Stede Bonnet lost his battle with Captain Rhett near the mouth of the river.

These pirates came upstream, out of reach of authorities, and supposedly settled between the Cape Fear and Black Rivers, near where Averasboro would later rise.

The first land grants that are known to have been issued inside present Harnett were given out in the early 1730s. The recipients included John Davis, Geoffrey Dawson, Richard French, and William Grey. All were located in the southeastern portion of the county, near the Cape Fear.

THE ARGYLL COLONY AND THE SCOTTISH SETTLERS

Though there were a few individuals residing in the bounds of modern Harnett by the 1730s, the most prolific group of people who settled the upper Cape Fear valley were the Highland Scots. Motivated by a sense of adventure and motivated to take bold steps because of economic and social chaos at home, the Scots found a place in the Sandhills of North Carolina where they could thrive.

Here, a man who might never have the opportunity to own a single acre of land in the "old country" could obtain up to 640 acres of woods and hills just by the asking, provided the correct paperwork was filed and a few minor improvements made on the tract.

Scottish immigration to the upper Cape Fear began as a small trickle in the 1720s and eventually increased to a flood by the time the American Revolution broke out, when the gates were temporarily closed. Though these men and women resumed their migration to North Carolina after the war, the pace never matched that of the half-century prior to 1776.

In the year 1736, Neal McNeal, Duncan Campbell, Dugald McNeal, Daniel McNeal, and Coll McAllister arrived at Brunswick Town near the mouth of the Cape Fear. They were in North Carolina looking for a suitable place to establish a colony for settlers from the Argyll region of Scotland. After receiving a cordial welcome from Governor Gabriel Johnston, they proceeded up the river in search of vacant land.

These individuals traveled as far up as Mermaid's Point. Along the way, they located several attractive sites and later filed grants for many of these prime tracts. They even bestowed their names on several creeks and other landmarks in what is now Harnett.

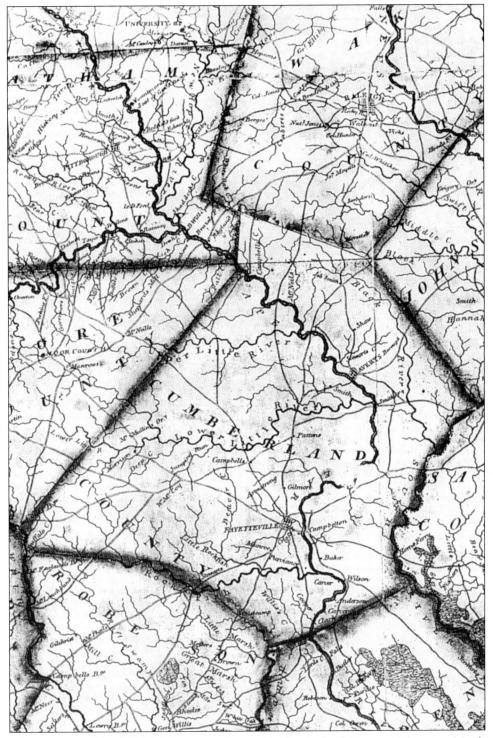

This portion of the 1833 McRae map shows old Cumberland County. (Courtesy North Carolina Department of Archives and History.)

The remains of John McAlester's gristmill are still visible in Bumpas Creek. The mill was constructed c. 1740, and the town of Averasboro grew up around it.

In 1739, the first group of colonists set sail from western Scotland, bound for North Carolina. They were the first in a long line of Scottish settlers known collectively as the Argyll Colony.

In its early stages, the Argyll Colony was concentrated along the Cape Fear in the vicinity of the Bluff in Cumberland County. But settlers continued on upriver. John McAlester, Dushee Shaw, Dugald Stewart, Patrick Stewart, Matthew Smylie, Nathaniel Smylie, and Samuel McGaw all took up land in 1740 near the present town of Erwin. Further upstream, individuals such as Gilbert Patterson, Archibald Buie, Hugh McCranie, and Neill McCranie settled.

In a letter written home in December of 1739, one of these settlers described the land they had found. He noted that the Cape Fear was, "navigable 140 miles up and plentiful for fish and the country abounding in wild cows of a large kind, plenty of deer, bear, wild geese, that the sd. Colony keep in a body, that they have no fear of the Indians." The mention of "wild cows of a large kind" was a description of the wild buffalo that once roamed central North Carolina before being driven west by the advance of settlement.

EARLY COUNTY FORMATION

In 1729, the southern portion of the province was designated as New Hanover County. New Town, later known as Wilmington, was the county seat. As settlers continued moving into the region, it became necessary to create yet another county, so in 1734, Bladen County was carved from New Hanover. This new county was quite large, stretching west from Livingston's Creek "to the bounds of Government." Old Bladen contained land that is today a part of 55 North Carolina counties and the entire state of Tennessee. In the east, the boundary of Bladen ran upstream from the mouth of Black River up the main branch of the river to its fork, "then the Westernmost Branch be the bounds to the Head thereof." This means that the land currently included in Harnett east of Black River would have remained a part of New Hanover County.

In the year 1750, Duplin County was formed from New Hanover. The western boundary line for the new county ran from where Six Runs and Coharie meet up the latter stream, "to the Head thereof." This left much of present Sampson, Harnett, and Cumberland Counties in New Hanover.

The fact that so many inhabitants had been left out of Duplin led Colonial officials to attempt to rectify the situation, so they shifted Duplin's boundary west in 1751. The new line ran west from the junction of Six Forks and Coharie directly to Black River, then upstream to the mouth of "Black Minge, thence up the said creek to the bounds of the said county." This helped many folks living in what is today Sampson, but for those who resided in what is now Harnett there would be no remedy until 1754.

As time passed and settlers continued moving into the backcountry of North Carolina, the administration of Bladen became quite cumbersome. Colonial officials found it necessary to begin carving out new counties from Bladen in order to provide adequate law enforcement and other necessary government services.

In 1750, the western half of Bladen was hewed away and formed into a new county known as Anson. Two years later, the northern portions of Bladen were included in a new county known as Orange. Then, in 1754, the northern half of what remained of Bladen was severed, and a new county formed known as Cumberland.

As it originally stood, Cumberland's southern boundary was on Cross Creek, well north of where it is today, while its northern boundary ran along the present Harnett/Wake line, bisected modern Lee and ran west along the northern boundary of Moore County. Hence, the geographic center of old Cumberland would have been roughly in the area between the two Little Rivers.

This county was named in honor of the Duke of Cumberland, the same duke who had been such a fierce and brutal enemy to the Scots during the 1745 Uprising, many of whom were resident in the Cape Fear Valley in the 1750s. Thus, he was not a popular man among the inhabitants of this area. The duke was loved by many in the Hanoverian side of the monarchy, so much so that a flower was named in his honor, "Sweet William." For many years, like other Scots around the globe, the folks in Harnett and the Carolina Sandhills often referred to this flower by its other name, "Stinking Billy."

The center of population was located along the Cape Fear between Bluff and Smiley's Falls, and when Cumberland's first sheriff, Bluff Hector McNeill, compiled a list of taxables in the 2,300 square miles of old Cumberland in 1755, he found "302 Whites, 11 Mullattoes and 63 Negroes."

In the spring of 1755 the first justices of Cumberland met at Justice Thomas Armstrong's house on the River Road near the present community of Slocumb to carry out Section VI of the law establishing the county, which directed that they were to "nominate and appoint a certain Place for building a Court-house, Prison and Stocks, as near as may be to the Centre of the said county."

The other justices present, Gilbert Clark and William Dawson, agreed to locate the seat of government on a tract of land Armstrong happened to own on the south side of Lower Little River near its confluence with the Cape Fear. The site chosen lay at what was then a veritable hub of transportation for the area, as most travelers utilized the waterways, which were tributaries of the Cape Fear, for transportation.

In addition, two popular land-based thoroughfares converged at the town, the River Road and the well-traveled Green's Path to the Pee Dee.

What made the site especially attractive to Dawson was the fact that he owned the ferry across the Cape Fear along the trail leading through town to South Carolina. His father Geoffrey had settled at this strategic crossing in 1737, and the ferry had been in operation long before Cumberland came into existence. The Dawsons also operated a tavern on the east side of the river to accommodate travelers.

Soon another ferry was needed to serve the fledgling town. On January 20, 1756 the justices empowered John Brown to operate a ferry over Lower Little River for the convenience of those coming down from the north. As a gesture of goodwill, the justices decreed that the ride should be free for those with court business.

The town that grew up around the courthouse was known as Chafferington, or Choeffington. The odd name is derived from a word that is seldom used today—chaffer, which means to bargain or haggle. An apt name for an eighteenth-century county seat and trading center.

The court that met here on the banks of Lower Little River was a powerful body in Colonial times, just as other county courts were throughout the Colony. Known as the Court of Pleas and Quarter Sessions because they convened four times per year, this body had the responsibility of administering and regulating the affairs of the county, as well as maintaining order.

They were, in modern terms, a board of commissioners and county manager rolled into one. Anything from punishment of minor offenses to maintaining standards of weights and measures to recording livestock brands and marks came under their jurisdiction.

The Scottish heroine Flora MacDonald is said to have attended services at Barbecue Presbyterian Church, as depicted in this painting by Eleanor Abbot. (Courtesy Presbyterian Historical Society.)

SECOND WAVE OF SCOTTISH MIGRATION

According to historian Duane Meyer, large influxes of Scottish Highlanders into North Carolina occurred in 1733, 1735, 1740, and 1753. "Before 1753," he writes, "the highland migration was sporadic." This trend of sporadic immigration continued until the late 1760s when large numbers of Highlanders were compelled to move to America due to adverse economic conditions in their homeland. This large influx continued until emigration was suspended with the coming of the American Revolution.

Many of the Scots making up the final pre–Revolutionary War influx to North America settled within the current bounds of Harnett. They were especially prevalent in the areas west of Cape Fear, where for years afterwards their native Gaelic language was frequently heard.

As their lives became more settled, many of the settlers desired to reacquaint themselves with their religious practices. A few missionaries preached in the area, but most met with limited success amongst the Scots due to the language barrier. One persistent Baptist minister who left his mark on Harnett was named

A memorial cairn marks the site of the original Barbecue Presbyterian Church.

Anderson. A large creek in what is now the southern part of the county carries his name, as he often utilized the stream as a guide through the vast longleaf pine forest through which no roads penetrated at the time.

The Presbyterians were more successful. In the year 1755, the Reverend Hugh McAden traveled south out of Pennsylvania to preach to the Ulster Scots who were settling in North Carolina. Hearing of the Scottish Highlanders settled on the Cape Fear, McAden decided to pay them a visit while he passed through the area. On January 26–27, 1756, he made his only stop within the present bounds of Harnett at David Smith's plantation, which was located on the west side of the Cape Fear between the two Little Rivers. In his journal McAden recorded, "On Tuesday, preached to a considerable number of people who came to hear me at Smith's."

When McAden returned to Pennsylvania he convinced Reverend James Campbell to journey to North Carolina and minister to the Scottish Highlanders. Reverend Campbell was uniquely qualified for the task, for not only was he a competent Presbyterian preacher, he also had the ability to speak English and Gaelic.

In addition, he had a friend already in residence in the area by the name of John Dobbin, who had been living since 1750 near Barbecue Creek along the road connecting Cross Creek and Hillsborough. Reverend Campbell utilized Dobbin's Ordinary, or tavern, as a convenient spot to hold religious services, and he possibly lived there until he could decide whether he wanted to make the move to North Carolina a permanent one.

Eventually, the congregation that came to hear Reverend Campbell preach at Dobbin's Ordinary decided to erect a permanent church building, which they did in the 1760s. According to church historian Reverend James MacKenzie, "It was not until 1765 or 1766 that a permanent place to worship was erected. This was a plain, unpretentious log building, but twenty-seven feet square, and unencumbered with flying buttresses, grinning gargoyles and lofty steeple." From these humble beginnings grew Barbecue Presbyterian Church, the oldest organized, active church within the bounds of Harnett County.

Perhaps the most prominent of the Scots arriving in the 1770s was Flora MacDonald, who had gained notoriety by aiding the Bonnie Prince Charlie in his flight from authorities following the defeat of the Jacobites at Culloden in 1746. Flora and her husband Allen MacDonald sailed to North Carolina in the fall of 1774. They initially lived with the family of Flora's half-sister Annabella at their plantation on Cameron's Hill.

Annabella was married to Alexander MacDonald of Cuidrach. Alexander had purchased the 100 acres upon which he built his plantation from Duncan Buie and his wife Sarah on July 10, 1772. The price for this piece of property on the south side of what was then known as Mount Pleasant was £80.

Flora remained at Mount Pleasant while her husband and son-in-law traveled through the western reaches of the Scottish settlement looking for an appropriate place to live. To pass the time, she often walked down the hill to the spring where she would sit on a rock smoking her clay pipe, looking to the west, and awaiting her husband's return. Ever since, the spring has been called the Flora MacDonald Spring and is a prominent Harnett County landmark.

Allan and Flora settled on a suitable site he had found on Cheeks Creek in what is today Montgomery County. But Flora's days of peace in North Carolina were short-lived, and most of her time in the state was met with hardships and adversity. This was due to the prominent part played by her husband in the Moore's Creek campaign in 1776. Following the debacle, one need only have been seen in Flora's company to be labeled a Tory. In the face of persecution, she left North Carolina and joined her husband, first in New York, then in Nova Scotia. Following the war, they returned to Scotland, having suffered much for the monarchy Flora had gained fame resisting in her youth.

REVOLUTIONARY WAR

When war broke out with the mother country, the allegiances of the inhabitants of Old Cumberland were greatly divided. A majority of the inhabitants, especially among the Scots, remained loyal to Great Britain. The rest were about equally divided between those who united with the Whigs and those who chose neutrality.

Action within the present bounds of Harnett began early in the war. On March 11, 1776, a force of 800 Loyalists was captured at Smith's Ferry on the Cape Fear River. This was the remnant of the army of Scots that had encountered the Whigs at Widow Moore's Creek on February 27, 1776.

Hugh MacDonald, who as a young boy was a participant in the Battle at Widow Moore's Creek, left an account of his flight from the field, up through what is now Sampson County to Mingo Swamp, where he and his fellow soldiers were captured by a force of Whig cavalry. MacDonald recalled the events that transpired at Smith's Ferry.

> This body of horsemen went on with us, considering us as their prisoners, to Smith's Ferry, where the flat being on the other side of the river, we were detained until this small party of horsemen received a reinforcement of about five hundred, when our waggons and every thing were taken from us, the men searched, and their ammunition was all taken from them. Though a boy, I did not escape the search; nor was I without ammunition; for a certain Malcolm Morrison had a large powder horn, which he slipped into the seat of my old buckskin breeches, which was very large, and a long hunting shirt hung over it. This was found and taken, which had like to have cost me trouble; for when my father learned that it was found with me, he flew at me to beat me; but a gentleman interfered, and the case being inquired into, I escaped my drubbing. Morrison had not less than a horse load of valuable plunder, of every kind, which he was allowed to carry home;

and by speculating on the proceeds of it, he laid a foundation of a tolerable estate.

We all got passports and were permitted to return home, except our officers who were taken prisoners and sent to Philadelphia, where they lay in jail until they were exchanged, but still getting their full pay from his Britannic Majesty, while we were justly hissed at for our incredulity, and were in danger from the citizens, who only a short time before, when we were without house or home, had kindly received us into their hospitality and friendship; but notwithstanding this scouring and the just contempt of our fellow citizens, we remained at heart as stiff Tories as ever.

Smylie's Falls are at the mouth of Upper Little River.

Whig forces under Colonel Caswell ranged through the Sandhills in a show of force they hoped would intimidate the Scottish Loyalists. They arrived at Barbecue Church on a Sunday and arrested several purported Loyalists, including the Reverend John McLeod, shortly after the services were concluded. It should be noted that many members of the Barbecue congregation were supporters of the Whig cause and remained such throughout the war despite the loyalty to the Crown on the part of their neighbors.

The most prominent Whig leaders who resided in what is now Harnett were Colonels David Smith and Ebeneazor Folsome. Smith's role in the war is unclear, but he is known to have been an important messenger for the Whig authorities. He lived in what historian Malcolm Fowler claimed was the first brick house

This is the final resting place of Revolutionary War hero Cornelius Harnett, namesake of Harnett County.

erected in Harnett, which stood off present N.C. Route 217 between Erwin and Linden. He was buried there in the family cemetery upon his death, but his remains were removed to the south side of Lower Little River to Sardis Church Cemetery, and thus now rest in Cumberland County.

More is known of his counterpart's career. Colonel Folsome lived on a large plantation that included the land on which now stands the Harnett County Government Complex north of Lillington. Folsome was a native of Connecticut who moved into the Cape Fear Valley in 1772, where he eventually acquired more than 4,000 acres of land. Beginning in 1774 he operated a tavern from his home, which stood along the King's Highway. This was a popular meeting place for Whigs and Tories alike, which made Folsome's Tavern a sort of neutral ground.

Folsome's Tavern was the site of one of the most widely known events in the annals of the Revolutionary War in the local area. Loyalist captain John MacNeill spent a day visiting with Colonel Folsome at his tavern before riding forth on a raid against some Whigs encamped at Piney Bottom. The Whigs in question had mistreated a young girl who lived near Anderson Creek as they passed through the area. Realizing he might have to stand trial some day for the actions about to transpire, MacNeill arranged the meeting with Folsome. MacNeill later used the meeting as an alibi, and his forethought gained him the name "Cunning John," as he escaped the hangman's noose after the war because a jury believed it impossible to ride the distance from Folsome's Tavern to Piney Bottom in the time allotted. "Cunning John" and his fellow Tories knew otherwise.

Colonel Folsome was an active leader. Most of his time during the war was spent rounding up Tories or guarding salt shipments. His most noteworthy achievement of the war came in August of 1776, when he was directed to proclaim the Declaration of Independence throughout the area. This was the first time that notable document had been heard in the upper Cape Fear country.

Following their initial successes in North Carolina, the Whigs saw fit to leave their wayward neighbors in peace, so long as they did not try to interfere with their revolution.

But they could not leave well enough alone, and in April of 1777 the Whig legislature passed an act that required everyone to take an "Oath of Allegiance" to the new government. This odd law was followed in November 1777 by the Confiscation Act, whereby those not taking the oath were subject to having their taxes tripled. If they failed to pay, the guilty person's property would be confiscated and sold to the highest bidder, the proceeds going to help fund the new government. Those whose property was seized were subsequently banished from the province.

Many refused to take the oath and suffered the consequences. But this odious law had an effect unforeseen by the Revolutionaries. The confiscation of people's homes and property led to outright hostility on the part of individuals who in all likelihood would have been content to let the Revolution take its course. Now there was a sizable portion of the population antagonistic to the Whig cause. Many traveled overland to Georgia and East Florida to join the Loyalist units such as the

This is the final resting place of Loyalist Colonel Archibald McDugald.

Royal North Carolina Regiment or Simcoe's Rangers. Some of the more vocal Loyalists were forced to take to the woods to escape persecution. Most waited, biding their time for the day of retribution that would surely follow once the lawful British authorities had restored order.

In April of 1781, Lord Cornwallis's army passed through what is now Harnett. Following the Battle of Guilford Courthouse, the British commander planned to move his weary army to Cross Creek, where he expected to find supplies and reinforcements, but circumstances necessitated that he continue with his troops down the Cape Fear to the British garrison at Wilmington.

Cornwallis's troops camped thrice in what is now Harnett, first near the present site of Mt. Pisgah Church, next at Barbecue Church, and finally in the extreme southern part of the county near Lower Little River. A brief skirmish was fought between local Whig militiamen and Colonel Banastre Tarleton's cavalry at the crossing over Upper Little River, the latter quickly overwhelming the Whigs and securing the crossing.

Following Cornwallis's passage through the area, the Loyalists who had heretofore kept a low profile began to rise and repay their Whig neighbors for past indignities. The guerrilla war that ensued is often referred to by historians as the Tory War and was a period of much violence and chaos for the people of central North Carolina. Several small, fierce encounters took place within what is now Harnett, but there were no large-scale battles fought within the bounds of the county.

Several Harnettians were present during the raid on Hillsborough in September of 1781, which was the most notable campaign of the Tory War. Loyalist forces under Colonel David Fanning raided Hillsborough on the morning of September 12, 1781. Fanning later wrote of the raid, "we killed 15 of the rebels and wounded 20. Also took upward of 200 prisoners. Amongst which was the Governor, his Councel, and part of the Continental Colonels, Several Captains and Subalterns & 71 Continental soldiers out of a Church."

Valuable prisoners in tow, including Whig governor Thomas Burke, the Loyalists set off for Wilmington, where Fanning planned to turn the captives over to Major James Craig, commander of the British garrison. The prisoners were put under the watchful eye of Captain "Sober John" McLean, who operated a gristmill on Upper Little River near where N.C. Route 210 currently crosses that watercourse. McLean was given the important responsibility because of his aversion to strong drink, which made him unlikely to get drunk and lose track of the prisoners.

On the morning of September 13, 1781, the Loyalist army was ambushed near the crossing of Cane Creek, and the Battle of Lindley's Mill ensued. After a fierce fight, the Loyalists prevailed and were able to proceed on their journey. Many prominent leaders had been incapacitated, including Colonel Fanning (wounded) and Colonel "Elder" Hector McNeill (killed). Command thus devolved upon Major Archibald McDugald, who through skill and audacity eluded Whig pursuers and deposited his valuable prisoners with Major Craig in Wilmington.

McDugald attained the rank of colonel before the war's end and has the distinction of being the highest ranking Loyalist officer from what is now Harnett. Prior to the war, he resided on a farm upstream from Clark's Bridge and had originally joined the Royal North Carolina Regiment in Savannah, Georgia, as an ensign. He later received a commission as major of the Cumberland County Loyalist Militia and usually operated as Colonel "Elder" Hector McNeill's second in command.

Following the war, McDugald was banished from North Carolina by the "Act of Pardon and Oblivion" because he had accepted the ensign's commission in the regular British army. He remained in Canada and England only a short while before returning to North Carolina and settling near the present site of Cameron, in Moore County. Upon his death, he was buried in the graveyard atop Cameron's Hill and has the distinction of being the highest ranking Revolutionary War officer, from either side, buried in a marked grave in the present bounds of Harnett.

3. THE FIRST SEVENTY YEARS OF INDEPENDENCE

On July 4, 1784, old Cumberland County was hewn in twain. The part lying northwest of "a line beginning at Cole's bridge on Drowning Creek thence a direct line to the corner of Wake and Johnston Counties in Cumberland line" was established as a new county called Moore. The new county was named for Alfred Moore, a prominent participant in the American Revolution. The portion of Cumberland southeast of the line was renamed Fayette County, in honor of the Marquis de Lafayette, of Revolutionary War fame.

Neither the new name for Cumberland nor the boundary with Moore lasted long. The boundary line as originally set forth gave the new county of Moore a large expanse of territory. Not only did it include present Moore and half of Lee, it included nearly half of what is now Harnett County as well. Losing such a large portion of its territory was not acceptable to the folks in Cumberland. The reason for their quarrel with the new name has not been recorded. To rectify the error, the General Assembly meeting at New Bern in October of 1784 amended the original act by shifting the Cumberland/Moore line west, to "begin at Cole's bridge, on Drowning Creek, thence a direct line to Cumberland and Chatham line, on south side of the river Cape Fear." The act also gave Cumberland back its old name.

FOUNDING OF OLD AVERASBORO

The first town officially incorporated within the bounds of what would become Harnett County was Averasboro, which had its official beginning in 1791 when the General Assembly, meeting in New Bern, approved its charter. The town, originally known as Averasburg, was surveyed and laid off in streets and lots on 120 acres of land donated by Alexander Avera. Serving as the first town commissioners were William Avera, Robert Draughon, Philemon Hodges, William Rand, and David Smith. A post office was established at Averasboro on October 1, 1794.

Averasboro grew quickly thanks to its strategic location, becoming the third largest town on the Cape Fear, trailing only Fayetteville and Wilmington. The town was situated at the head of pole boat navigation on the Cape Fear, at the foot of Smiley's Falls, and was thus a popular shipping point for those transporting goods upstream from Fayetteville. It was also a popular stopover point for those traveling downriver with log rafts loaded with naval stores that had been extracted from the longleaf pine forests in the upper Cape Fear valley. In addition, two important thoroughfares passed through town, the Raleigh-Fayetteville Stage Road and the King's Highway.

EARLY NAVIGATION SCHEMES FOR THE CAPE FEAR RIVER

The Cape Fear River in Harnett County is beset with numerous shoals and rapids. The largest of these was Buckhorn Falls on the Lee/Chatham/Harnett line and Smiley's Falls near Erwin. Of these, the most troublesome for engineers was the latter, as this was the place where a highly resistant vein of granite crossed the river. All of the falls in Harnett County were eventually overcome, but some only briefly.

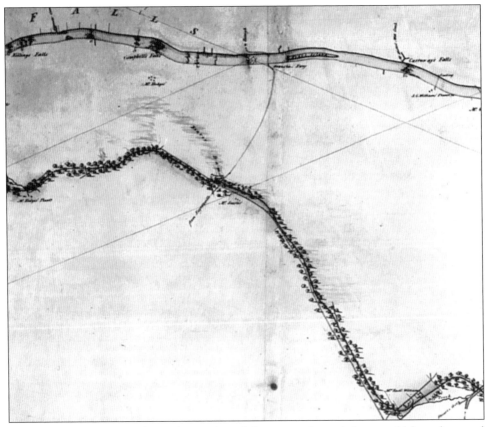

The 1822 Brazier map shows the portion of the proposed canal that would have bypassed Smylie's Falls and Averasboro.

Barclay's Inn at Barclaysville was once a popular stop along the Stage Road. (Courtesy North Carolina Department of Archives and History.)

Attempts to make the river navigable in Harnett date as far back as 1756, when justices for Cumberland County appointed four men to keep the river free of obstructions. This included removing such items as trees, stumps, or anything else that might snag the canoes and timber rafts that were the main forms of transportation on the river at the time.

The first company to be organized to improve the upper portions of the river for navigational purposes was the Cape Fear Company. Organized in 1792 by the state legislature, this group accomplished nothing of consequence.

Organized by the legislature in 1796, the Deep and Haw River Company was the next group to try to tame the upper reaches of the Cape Fear. This group attempted to dig canals around the rapids at Buckhorn and Smiley's Falls. At Smiley's Falls they started their canal below Bumpas Creek and followed the bluff on the east side of the river until workers encountered the vein of granite near Narrow Gap.

Their failure to penetrate the granite at Narrow Gap led to their demise. The remains of the canal are still visible in the woods near Narrow Gap.

The Cape Fear Navigation Company was the third organization to try to overcome the obstacles in the river. Organized in 1815, this group first proposed to bypass Smiley's Falls by a canal on the west side of the river from Fox Island near the present site of Lillington to Fayetteville. This was given up as too expensive, much to the relief of the Averasboro folks, who lived on the opposite side of the river and would have lost out on much commerce.

The Cape Fear Navigation Company decided to overcome the obstacles in the upper Cape Fear with wing dams built into the river and designed to direct the flow of water into natural sloughs at the end of the falls that the company improved and lined with rocks. These efforts were a limited success and allowed river transportation as far up as the Haw River during periods of high water.

One of the sites of more extensive navigational work was at Buckhorn, where a system of dams, locks, and canals were employed. Due to miscalculations on the part of engineers, these structures collapsed under the pressure of the water. The canal, part of which had originally been dug by the Deep and Haw River Company in the early 1800s, stretched from the head of the falls in Chatham County to Parker's Creek in Harnett County.

In addition to requiring constant upkeep, the wing dams were not able to stand up to the force of the floods, or freshets, that were once common on the Cape Fear and required almost constant upkeep. By the late 1820s, the Cape Fear Navigation Company gave up on the upper reaches of the river and concentrated on keeping the Cape Fear open between Fayetteville and Wilmington.

RALEIGH-FAYETTEVILLE STAGE ROAD

A road along the east side of the Cape Fear connecting Raleigh and Fayetteville became a very important transportation artery in the years following the Revolutionary War. This road, which cut across what is now Harnett, became a major link in the system of roads followed by government mail stages in the early nineteenth century. Historian John Oates wrote of this historic route: "The Fayetteville post office was one of the first post offices established and was on the original 'mail post road' from Scoodic, Maine to St. Mary's Ga., a distance of 1,765 miles. This was established in 1798. The North Carolina post offices served on this route were Warrenton, Louisburg, Raleigh, Averysborough, Fayetteville and Lumberton."

In 1818, state engineer Hamilton Fulton studied this road, which he called, "the greatest thoroughfare from South to North in the State of North Carolina." He was looking at ways to improve the state's transportation arteries, both on land and on the water, and his study of the Stage Road was aimed toward improving the road.

He was also looking at the feasibility of establishing a new route directly from Fayetteville to the Virginia border.

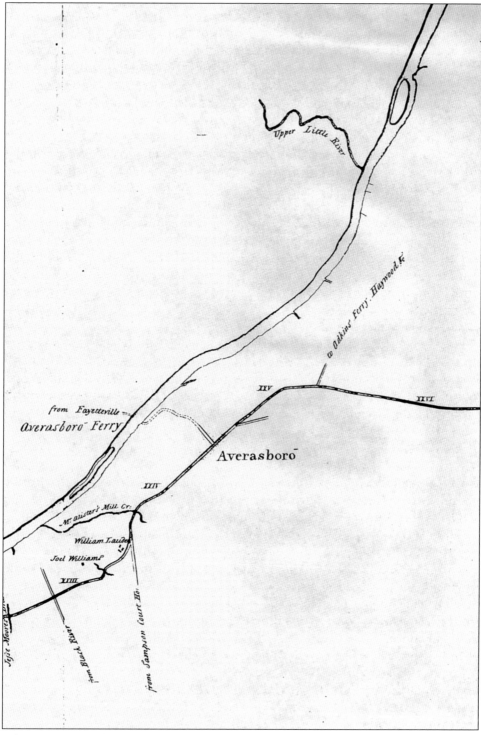

This section map of the stage road shows the vicinity of Averasboro. (Courtesy North Carolina Department of Archives and History.)

On a map accompanying his report, Fulton plotted several prominent landmarks in what is now Harnett. These included the Dushee Shaw Halfway House, a popular stopover on the road built equidistant from Raleigh and Fayetteville, and Barclays Inn, another popular stopping place for travelers along the stage road.

PLANK ROADS

In the year 1846, the State of North Carolina hired Dr. Elisha Mitchell to survey a route for turnpikes connecting Raleigh and Fayetteville with the western portions of the state. These roads were to have been little more than dirt thoroughfares but were considered a vast improvement over the roads then in use.

For the Fayetteville turnpike, Mitchell surveyed two potential routes to Salisbury, one that passed through Troy in Montgomery County and one that passed through Carthage and Asheboro.

In his report on the latter route, Mitchell commented upon the difficulties of crossing the Sandhills of what is today southwestern Harnett County.

> Through the greater part of 30 miles after we strike the sand, there is no road, but every person selects a route for himself, following the general course of previous travel along the ridge that separates the waters which flow into the Cape fear, from those that run into the two Peedees. It is in fact the old trail by which Buffaloes and Indians used to come down from the interior to the coast. One is often uncertain, whilst attempting to follow it, whether he is advancing towards the end of his journey, or merely crossing diagonally from one side of the ridge to the other.

Dr. Mitchell's turnpikes were never constructed, as the project never received the support of the business leaders of Fayetteville, many of whom were ardent supporters of a railroad leading west from Fayetteville, which Dr. Mitchell did not support. Thus, it appeared that the advocates of improving transportation into the western and central reaches of the state were at an impasse.

Fortunately, there was a solution, which came by way of the frozen north. In the 1830s, in the forests of Russia and Canada, a new form of road building had been developed to provide a reliable road surface across difficult terrain. These roads were built of wood, and thus dubbed "plank roads." Many looked to them as an economical alternative to the high costs associated with railroad construction.

THE FAYETTEVILLE AND WESTERN PLANK ROAD

In January of 1849, the Fayetteville and Western Plank Road Company was chartered to construct a plank road from Fayetteville to Salisbury. Several prominent business leaders from Old Cumberland were present.

Work was slow at first, as the company officials and engineers had never before engaged in building a wooden road. Therefore the first 12.8-mile section of the road from Fayetteville to Manchester was a grand experiment, opening for travel, with toll booths in place, in April of 1850. Over the next section of the road, from Little River to Carthage, work dragged on until September 1, 1850, when the road was finally opened beyond Carthage. The total cost of constructing the road from Fayetteville to Carthage was $61,677.15.

Beyond the Moore County seat, the temporary terminus of the road was at Johnsonville in Randolph County (not to be confused with Johnsonville in Harnett County). This section was contracted in July of 1850 to Jonathan Worth, who was to receive "$425 per mile for clearing, grading, planking and finishing." By March of 1852, Worth had completed his section, laying "45 miles, 4265 feet" of plank at a total cost of $8,577.56.

Beyond Johnsonville, the people of Salem finally raised enough funds to lure the Fayetteville and Western to their town instead of Salisbury. The road was extended all the way to Bethania in 1854. This made the total length of the Fayetteville and Western Plank Road 129 miles, to this day the longest wooden highway ever constructed.

"Ring Ear" Sam Johnson's inn stood along the Fayettville and Western Plank Road.

This milepost stood along the Fayetteville and Western Plank Road. The notches represent the mileage from Fayetteville. (Courtesy North Carolina Department of Archives and History.)

After these experimental beginnings, the design chosen for the plank road called for it to be built 8 feet wide. This was accomplished by first grading the roadway for good drainage, then laying four timbers or "stringers" lengthwise and connecting these with thick 5-by-8-foot planks. The ends of the planks were offset 4 inches every third plank, leaving a serrated pattern that allowed vehicles easy access back onto the road when they pulled off and hopefully would prevent ruts.

The final step in the construction of a plank road was to apply a covering of sand. The leading authority on road construction of the day gave the following reason for this. "The grit of the sand soon penetrates into the grain of the wood, and combines with the fibres, and the droppings upon the road, to form a hard and tough covering, like felt, which greatly protects the wood from the wheels and the horses' shoes."

Much of the hard, backbreaking work of constructing the road in Harnett County was initially performed by slaves working under the direction of the superintendent and engineers.

One enterprising individual was Major Dugald MacDugald, son of Colonel Archibald MacDugald. The young MacDugald rented slaves from several landowners in Cumberland and Moore Counties. Unfortunately, a typhoid outbreak in one of the camps killed all of the slaves working on the project. MacDugald lost his fortune after having to reimburse the slaveholders for the loss of their valuable property.

The Fayetteville and Western was a well-traveled thoroughfare: wagons full of agricultural products of the Piedmont and foothills of North Carolina rolled down the road to Fayetteville. They were laden with anything from apples to wheat. Great hogsheads of tobacco were transported down the plank road by having an axle placed lengthwise through the center, which were pulled along by horses and oxen in the same manner as a wagon.

Reports indicate that $26,796.73 were taken in tolls on the road for the year 1854, which was the peak usage of the road. Toll rates were 1¢ per mile for horseback riders, 1.5¢ per mile for one-horse wagons, 2¢ per mile for a two-horse team, 2.5¢ for a three-horse team, and 3¢ for a four-horse team. Tollhouses were constructed along the road at approximately 12 mile intervals. The only tollhouse located in Harnett County was constructed on Round Top, west of Cameron's Hill, 24 miles from Fayetteville.

The land was given by A.J. Cameron, Esq. and the cost of building the structure was $270. Malcolm Clark served as the first toll collector at Round Top. Upon his resignation in 1852, he was replaced by Martin Bolton. The toll keeper's salary at Round Top was $100 per year.

Land prices along the route soared, and new businesses sprang up as employment opportunities rose and new money flowed into the community. An editorial in the April 16, 1851 issue of the *Fayetteville Observer* notes, "the increase in the value of land between this place and Carthage, has been more than the whole cost of the road between those points."

Unfortunately, the days of prosperity for the Fayetteville and Western were short lived. Few of the road's early advocates had foreseen the high maintenance costs associated with a wooden highway. The heavy flow of traffic quickly wore out the planks, which by necessity had to be replaced, as holes in plank roads were extremely hazardous to four-legged beasts.

The company tried several ways to improve the road in an economical and efficient manner, but none were successful. The efforts to repair the road were hampered by numerous financial problems, which included the decrease in toll revenue as more and more farmers in the Piedmont opted to utilize the North Carolina Railroad to get their crops to market. This road of iron, though more expensive to construct, was more durable and therefore a more reliable mode of transportation. Plus, the Panic of 1857 limited the amount of capital available to investors to put into such projects.

With the outbreak of the War between the States, most of the road fell into disrepair and the toll booths were removed, especially after the General Assembly gave the company permission to abandon any section so long as no tolls were collected along that stretch. Thus did the Fayetteville and Western Plank Road fade into oblivion.

OTHER PLANK ROADS

Several other plank roads that would have traversed the county were planned. In May of 1851, subscription books were opened across central North Carolina to sell an additional $100,000 in stock for the Fayetteville and Western Plank Road Company. At Summerville, the Reverend Simeon Coulton, Alexander McLean, and John McKay directed the sale. Any funds taken in at Summerville were to be used specifically for the survey and construction of a branch line of the Fayetteville and Western from a point "14 miles from Fayetteville" to the Cape Fear River via Summerville. Upon reaching the river the company planned to construct a bridge. There is no evidence the company ever built this spur line, but a map of Toomer drawn in 1855 gives evidence that the route was in fact surveyed, if not fully constructed.

Another plank road that was slated to cross Harnett was never completed. The Fayetteville and Raleigh Plank Road was chartered as a joint stock company by the legislature in December 1852. According to an article in the January 1, 1853 *North Carolinian*, the line had been completed 11 miles north of Fayetteville to a settlement known as Kingsbury, in northern Cumberland County near the present town of Linden. The remarkable speed of construction demonstrates that the company was at work on the line before the charter was granted.

At the first meeting of the board of directors of the Fayetteville and Raleigh, Henry Elliott was elected president and Archibald McLean was chosen as secretary/treasurer. A route had been surveyed as far north as McNeill's Ferry, but the records are unclear if any planks were laid that far north. By November of 1853, the company had taken in enough tolls to pay an 8 percent dividend. But growth of this company was stymied by the lack of interest shown on the part of investors in Raleigh, so the Fayetteville and Raleigh Plank Road became a local line serving the people between Fayetteville and McNeill's Ferry.

Of these plank road ventures, only one was known to have been built into Harnett. In January of 1851, the Fayetteville and Northern Plank Road Company was chartered by the General Assembly. Their purpose was to build a plank road connecting Raleigh and Fayetteville. They were also authorized to build a branch to Smithfield. The most northern point reached, however, was Averasboro.

CAPE FEAR AND DEEP RIVER NAVIGATION COMPANY

In the year 1848, the Cape Fear and Deep River Navigation Company was organized to tame the mighty Cape Fear above Fayetteville, providing a reliable transportation outlet for the mineral resources of the Deep River country, as well as the agricultural commodities of Cumberland and Chatham Counties.

Work got underway in 1848 with a reconnaissance survey of the rivers by William B. Thompson, chief engineer. Construction of a system of locks and dams at several of the rapids along the river began in 1849. The quality of the

The remains of the lock system in the Cape Fear River are visible at Northington Falls.

engineering of these navigational works was greatly improved over earlier attempts to overcome the obstacles in the river. The crib dams packed with rock were improved to make them more resistant to the pressures of the river.

The project was completed by 1856. Ten of the lock and dam sites were located in Harnett County. These included Battles Lock and Dam; Douglass Falls, or Northington Lock and Dam; McAlister's Lock and Dam; Sharpfield's Lock and Dam; Big Island Lock and Dam; Green Rock Lock and Dam; Haw Ridge Lock and Dam; and Red Rock Lock and Dam. Though these structures were much more durable than their predecessors had been, they were still prone to damage from floodwaters, especially when the river went on a rampage, such as the one occurring in September of 1856.

The company managed to keep the river open to steamboats throughout the 1850s, with numerous boat landings on the river. The increase in riverborne transport led to a boom period for old Averasboro, as commerce rose steadily and the town began to grow. But the steam transportation on the river ended following the damage to the locks and dams below Northington Falls during freshets in 1859 and 1860. As the company was engaged in repairing the damage, the War between the States began, bringing the work to a halt. Following the war, it was never again found to be economically feasible to open the upper Cape Fear for navigational purposes. The exception to this was the works from Battles Lock and Dam upstream to Deep River in Chatham County. This section of the river was kept open through the War between the States and into the 1870s to provide transport for the iron of Buckhorn to the railhead at Egypt.

WESTERN RAILROAD

On Christmas Eve of 1852, the Western Railroad received its charter from the state. The purpose of the organization was to build a rail line connecting Fayetteville with the Deep River coal fields at Egypt in Chatham County. For the first five years of its existence the company purchased right of way along its route and did not begin actual work on the ground until the spring of 1858. By the end of the year, tracks had been laid for 11 miles northwest of Fayetteville, and by the end of 1859 tracks were extended north into Harnett to a siding known as Flee Hill, whose name was officially changed to Pineview in 1906. By 1861, the 43-mile line was completed all the way to the Egypt Coal Mine. The total cost for the project was $1,025,016, which works out to roughly $24,000 per mile.

Labor for the project was provided mostly by Irish immigrants; local contractors had learned their lesson from Major McDugald's plight when the valuable slaves he had contracted to work on the plank road had succumbed to a typhoid outbreak. Since the Irishmen did not actually belong to anyone, they were thus considered to be more expendable than local slaves. A similar view was adopted by contractors on the navigational improvements on the river, who normally opted for Irish or Italian immigrants to fill their labor needs. A camping place just east of Summerville is still known as Italy Hill.

In November of 1859 a writer for the *Fayetteville Observer* described the depot at Spout Springs as "a handsome and commodious depot building." Spout Springs was an important site along the line. The plank road, which ran on the eastern side of the rails and paralleled it north of Little River, crossed over the tracks on a wooden bridge and headed northwest at Spout Springs. It was envisioned that many farmers would be tempted to travel down the plank road as far as Spout Springs where their goods would be disposed of to middlemen who would in turn ship the goods on the railroad to market at Fayetteville. Such plans never materialized, though in later years Spout Springs did become an important point in the shipment of naval stores extracted from the longleaf pine forests of the Sandhills of western Harnett.

In addition to Spout Springs, several other communities grew up along the Western Railroad. These include Swann's Station, Rock Branch/Olivia, and Pineview. Just east of the route of the Western Railroad was Buffalo Springs, an important trading settlement that served as a naval stores shipping point for the folks in the region prior to the construction of the plank road and railroad. But due to its lack of adequate transportation, the settlement could not compete with those along the railroad, and faded away, reportedly meeting its demise in 1865 when Yankee troops burned what was left of the place to the ground. But Buffalo Springs did have one claim to fame. It was the home of the county's first published newspaper and magazine. Handwritten by John McLean Harrington, *The Nation* and *The Young American* both began at Buffalo Springs in 1858.

This "Chatham" 4-4-0 locomotive that ran on the Western Railroad between Fayetteville and Egypt was photographed at Baldwin Locomotive Works c. 1866. (Courtesy North Carolina Department of Archives and History.)

4. Founding of Harnett

The people of the extreme northern portion of Cumberland County began agitating to form their own county in the early 1800s. In 1829 Archibald McDiarmiad, one of their representatives in the House of Commons, presented the General Assembly with a petition for the creation of a new county. The proposed county was to have been called Jackson and would include portions of Cumberland, Wake, Chatham, and Moore Counties. The bill passed on its first reading and was sent to the Committee of Propositions and Grievances to work out the details. But the bill never emerged from committee, and thus Jackson died a premature death.

Other attempts to create a new county for these people were made between 1829 and 1850, with the most vigorous one coming in 1844. In that year, the attempt was to create a new county called Blakely, in honor of Captain Johnston Blakely, a hero of the War of 1812 and former Pittsboro resident. But this attempt, though popular with the populace, suffered the same fate as did its predecessors.

Legislation Creating Harnett County

Ten years would pass before the people of northern Cumberland would get a legitimate chance to go their own way. This was becoming a very important issue to those living on the north and east side of the river above the town of Averasboro. Their cause was helped in 1854 with the election of a young man to the House of Commons who was both sympathetic to their views and naive about the world of politics. C.H. Coffield, who lived near what is now the community of Chalybeate Springs, was elected from Cumberland along with Malcolm J. McDuffie and Jesse Shepherd. The latter gentlemen's loyalties were clearly with the moneyed interest in Fayetteville, but not so with Coffield.

When the three men took their seats in the House of Commons on November 20, 1854, appearances led one to assume that nothing out of the ordinary would occur in that august body during that session. After taking care of some routine business, they would soon be home for the holidays.

These dreams were dashed in the fall of 1854 when the young Coffield stood up and introduced a bill to create Henry County from not just the northern tip of

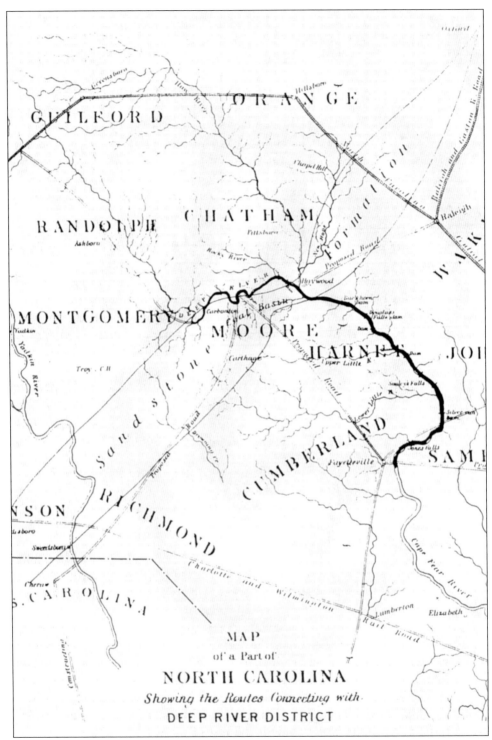

This earliest-known map of Harnett, which shows various routes to the Deep River coal fields, was made shortly after the county was created.

Cumberland, but the entire northern half of Cumberland lying above Lower Little River. Coffield emphasized the need for a new county by pointing out that it was only 12 miles from the courthouse in Fayetteville to the Robeson County line, but over 45 miles to the Wake County line.

In what must have seemed a strange turn of events, Coffield's colleague from Cumberland, Sheppard, was the first to stand and speak against the measure, and he would prove to be the most vocal opponent. He stated that this was the first he had heard of any dissatisfaction with local government from the people and claimed that it was nothing more than a scheme by "certain individuals" to grab power. His main point, though, was that he first heard of Coffield's bill along with the rest of the House of Commons, and he chastised Coffield for the discourtesy of not discussing the matter with his colleagues first.

That the idea was all part of a scheme by "certain individuals" as Sheppard suggested is probably very close to the truth, but Coffield was being manipulated by more than just local interests back home. After all, the man he replaced in the House, George W. Pegram, lived even further from Fayetteville than did Coffield, but he did not try to lead a secession movement. In all likelihood, Coffield was being used by members of the General Assembly in the struggle to shift the balance of power in the state by creating new counties, thus adding seats to the General Assembly. Hence, the measure flew through the House with relative speed.

A major hurdle for the effort stood in the State Senate, where the measure could be crushed with ease by Cumberland's State Senator Warren Winslow. This Fayetteville lawyer and former merchant was a relative novice in the political arena but was so well liked by his peers that they chose him to be Speaker of the Senate shortly after he took office in 1854.

But Winslow was more than merely Speaker of the Senate. In the fall of 1854, Governor David Settle Reid was elected to the U.S. Senate and, therefore, resigned from the office of governor. This move elevated Winslow to governor, and he served concurrently in the two offices thanks to a decision reached in the General Assembly stating that such an act was legal.

Thus, Winslow was a busy man when the question of dividing his home county came up. Perhaps this is why he did not aggressively fight the measure. But the bill's supporters needed to make sure the powerful senator had an incentive not to oppose the new county.

To accomplish this, someone lay hold of a brilliant idea. When the new county came into being, the town named as the county seat would be called Toomer, in honor of Judge John D. Toomer, formerly of Fayetteville but living in 1854 in retirement in Pittsboro. Judge Toomer was a very popular jurist, but most important in this instance was the fact that he was also Warren Winslow's father-in-law. Thanks to this appeal to Winslow's familial connections, the measure creating the new county easily made it the rest of the way through the General Assembly. Save for a couple of name changes, the measure passed and was ratified by a 2-to-1 margin on February 7, 1855.

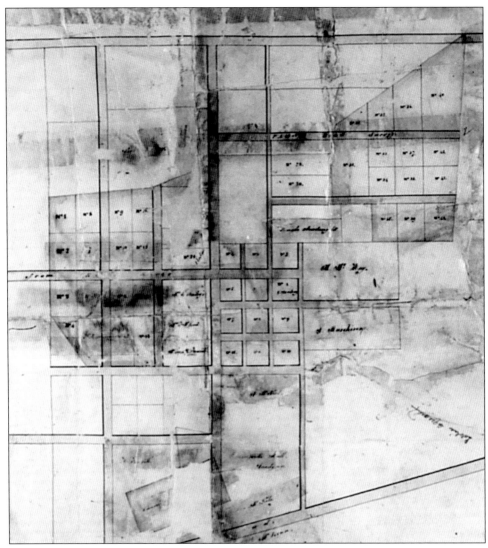

This map of Toomer shows the layout of Harnett's first county seat. (Courtesy North Carolina Department of Archives and History.)

Ironically, the new county ended up being called Harnett, in honor of Revolutionary War hero Cornelius Harnett. This has led to some speculation that C.H. Coffield had pulled a prank on the General Assembly and named the county for himself, as his full name was Cornelius Harnett Coffield. Alas, this myth is not supported by fact, for when Coffield put forth the bill he named the new county Henry for Judge Louis D. Henry. An amendment changed this to Cape Fear, and finally another amendment was put forth to change the name to Harnett. The Harnett name was offered up by Thomas Settle, representative of Rockingham County.

Another important fact to note is that not all of the inhabitants of the new county wanted to be severed from old Cumberland. Sheppherd gathered 600 signatures from within the affected area on a petition opposing the act, but presented it too late to have any effect on the General Assembly's decision.

The act creating Harnett contained little practical material about setting up a new government, so a supplemental act was passed on February 15, 1855. This act covered the workings of the new county's government in detail, setting up courts, naming commissioners to mark boundaries, making provisions for collecting taxes, and so forth.

TOOMER, THE FIRST COUNTY SEAT

Section 7 of the Supplemental Act named George W. Pegram, John Green, Eldridge Stewart, James Johnson, James P. Hodges, John McKay, and Sam Johnson as commissioners to locate a site for the town of Toomer, which at that point existed on paper only. The group had much leeway in regards to how they acquired the land, but the provision was very specific in one matter—the county seat of Harnett had to be "at or within three miles of the geographical center." As soon as a site was chosen for Toomer, the specifics of laying out the town were to be carried out. This was covered in Section 8, which read as follows:

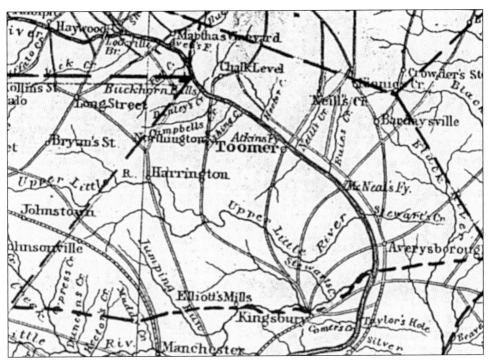

This portion of the 1865 Coast Survey Map of North Carolina shows Toomer's prominence in the 1850s prior to the creation of Lillington.

BE IT FURTHER ENACTED, That the county court of Harnett, at its first session after the site for the county town shall have been determined, shall appoint five commissioners to lay off the lots of said town and to designate public squares; and the said commissioners shall expose to sale, at public auction, the said lots, retaining such as, in their judgement, may be needed for county purposes, for churches and academies, taking bond and security for purchase money, and such terms of credit as the county court, a majority of the justices being present, shall direct. The bonds shall be made payable to the chairman of the county court, who, or his successors, shall execute deeds to the purchasers, which shall be available in law to pass the title; and the proceeds of the sale shall be applied to the erection of public buildings.

Immediately after passage of the act creating Harnett, the seven commissioners met at Cumberland Academy. Their first order of business was to locate the geographic center of the county, and to do this they brought along David McDuffie, a noted topographer from Fayetteville.

McDuffie had been prominent in the region as a mapmaker and surveyor, and one of his credits included a map for the Lower Little River and Crane's Creek Navigation Company. He also had drawn a map of Cumberland prior to the split.

When presented with the problem of finding the center of Harnett County, McDuffie decided that a whole new survey was not in order. Instead, he made the calculations from charts and maps he had previously compiled. When he was finished, the center of the county was calculated to be a point approximately 1.5 miles south of Cumberland Academy on the Johnsonville Road. The point was later marked with a lightwood stump.

The commissioners decided that since the village of Summerville with its fine roads and educational facilities was within the prescribed 3-mile zone, they would merely lay out their town there. They presented their findings to the Harnett officials' first gathering, which was held at the Cumberland Academy on March 11, 1855.

No objections to the chosen site were made, and the commissioners locating the site for the county seat quickly moved to secure title to the necessary land about Summerville. Most came from the Reverend Neill McKay and his brother Dr. John McKay, and in a gesture of philanthropy, Henry Faucette donated 30 acres. The land was presented to the justices at the June 1855 session of the court.

Not everyone believed the commissioners had acquired the best of land for the county seat. In 1927 County Historian D.P. MacDonald noted, "Part of the land was like Bill Nye's perpendicular farm in Western North Carolina and was not considered suitable for the purpose intended. The impression prevailed that the school location was of first importance, and this caused a general dissatisfaction as to the location of the courthouse."

FIRST MEETING OF THE HARNETT JUSTICES

Until the public buildings could be erected, the Court of Pleas and Quarter Sessions was ordered to meet at the village of Summerville, where stood the Cumberland Academy, a renowned institute of higher learning. The academy was officially organized in 1846, and had once been under the direction of Dr. Simeon Coulton, a controversial Presbyterian teacher.

George W. Pegram was the first county official elected in Harnett in 1855, serving as chairman of the Court of Pleas and Quarter Sessions.

Summerville Presbyterian Church stands near the site of Summerville Academy, where the first meeting of Harnett officials took place in 1855.

The first meeting of the Harnett Court of Pleas and Quarter Sessions that convened at Summerville on March 11, 1855 went smoothly. As historian Malcolm Fowler pointed out, "This was the first and most harmonious political meeting ever held in Harnett County as such—a regular love feast, so to speak. It was probably the last, if we can rely on the records." The justices present elected George W. Pegram as chairman and James Banks as clerk pro temp. Additionally, the following selections were made: James A. Johnson, sheriff; Neill McKay, county solicitor; John L. Bethea, county trustee; Arch Bethea, county surveyor; Hector McLean, coroner; Jonathan Holly, entry taker; James T. Reardon, standard keeper; "Deaf" Duncan McLean, register of deeds; and B.F. Shaw, clerk of the court.

The most pressing item of business was to erect the edifices of county government. The justices accepted the report of the commission appointed by the General Assembly to locate a site for the county seat. Once the land was secured, the Building Committee made up of Dr. John McKay, James Hodges, and John W. McNeill set about the task of erecting the county buildings. This was a pressing matter not so much for the courthouse, as the officials could meet in the academy, but a jail was urgently needed. Prisoners were being kept in Cumberland until adequate facilities could be prepared in Harnett. At first this was an acceptable arrangement, as Harnett's Superior Court cases were to be tried in Cumberland until 1857. After that time, Harnett would be responsible for its own cases.

Pascal McKay was awarded the contract to build both the courthouse and jail at Toomer. The cost was $12,000 for the courthouse and $6,400 for the jail. This was, of course, a great deal more than the $10,000 that had been stipulated in the Supplemental Act as the amount the county could borrow for the erection of the public buildings. Payments were to be made on a quarterly basis: the first one was due when the building materials were put on the ground.

Pascal McKay wasted little time getting together his materials for the jail. He was so fast, in fact, that the county had not collected any taxes and therefore had no money on hand with which to pay him. To avoid a potentially embarrassing situation for the county, John McNeill, treasurer of the Building Committee, paid the first $1,500 from his own personal funds.

When the county courts met in the Summerville Academy (formerly named Cumberland Academy), Toomer became a lively place. To accommodate the schedule of the students, the justices chose Saturday as the day on which to transact the public's business. One day was usually more than enough to take care of the county's affairs. If perchance one needed to take care of some business at any other time, one merely visited the home of the county official needed.

Court days created an almost festive atmosphere, as inhabitants converged on the county seat for quarterly meetings that provided an opportunity to socialize and celebrate. This was attractive to those living on remote farms. Once official business was taken care of, people could spend the rest of the day talking with friends, fighting, horse racing, cock fighting, or buying goods from the traveling salesmen peddling their wares from the back of wagons. Liquor, conspicuously absent from the first gathering, eventually became a regular feature.

CONTROVERSY OVER THE COUNTY SEAT

Toomer was embroiled in controversy almost as soon as it came into existence. As stated earlier, several individuals did not think highly of the site chosen for the county seat, reasoning that the commissioners placed the utmost importance on placing the new town near Summerville Academy to promote that institution. There was also grumbling about honoring a lawyer from Fayetteville by naming their town for him.

James Johnson of Buie's Creek was Harnett's first sheriff.

Another reason for the disaffection with the county seat was its location so far away from the river crossings. When the river was high, crossing the Cape Fear was a perilous undertaking, and for those living on the opposite side of the river from Toomer this was a very real hardship.

Finally, there was the matter of selling land for the county seat. Those who had given or sold land to the commission wanted a reverter clause put in so they would get their land back in case the county should one day get rid of their holdings. The justices would not go for that. More importantly, though, was that people thought the landowners were engaging in some type of subterfuge and many were convinced that they would in a short time figure out a way to raise their prices.

All these things led toward a huge controversy that came to a head during the spring of 1856. The people of Harnett wanted to move the county seat.

Since the records for this period of Harnett's history are sparse, it is difficult to piece together what happened during the spring of 1856. What is known is that the populace had become so adamant about the county seat issue they were asking for a referendum to decide to move it. In light of this, the justices thought it would be foolish to spend money on the edifices of county government and then have the county seat move, so they discharged the building committee.

The main problem with this, of course, was the fact that Pascal McKay had already assembled the materials on the site and was almost finished with the jail. He therefore continued to work on the brick jailhouse, feeling that he would be paid as per his contract regardless of whether there was a Building Committee. The Harnett officials thought otherwise, and filed an injunction against McKay in May of 1856 to halt construction. They were too late, as by June he was finished and presented the county with a bill for his labors.

The officials were obstinate and decided not to levy a tax to raise money to pay for the construction. McKay promptly hauled them into court and won, the Superior Court in Cumberland County ruling in late June that the Harnettians had to levy a tax and pay off McKay for the work done. The decision was appealed in an effort to buy time to raise the money. The county lost again but managed to arrange a deal that allowed them to only pay McKay for the work completed prior to the elimination of the building committee. The total amount McKay was awarded was $6,000, less the $1,500 he had already collected.

To add insult to injury, the justices soon discovered that the jail they were being forced into buying was of shoddy workmanship. The first prisoner incarcerated there was George Ferguson, who escaped before breakfast on the morning after he was locked up. As Fowler noted, Ferguson "dug his way out through the soft brick and weak mortar as soon as he got sober enough to stand up."

As things turned out, Ferguson had the honor of being the only prisoner ever held in the old jail at Toomer. Following his escape, the sheriff decided that the jailhouse was not secure enough and continued sending prisoners to Fayetteville, an arrangement that would stay in effect until 1867.

One final note concerning the jail. In 1857, the treasurer of the Building Committee John McNeill, who had, in effect, lent the county the first $1,500 payment on construction costs for county facilities, passed away. He had been married to Rosanna Worth, daughter of Jonathan Worth of Randolph County, a prominent politician and superintendent for the Fayetteville and Western Plank Road Company. McNeill's father-in-law administered his estate and discovered the receipt from Pascal McKay for the aforementioned $1,500. Worth entered suit against the county and won, taking another chunk from Harnett's meager coffers. Incidentally, Worth would go on to serve as governor of North Carolina from 1865 through 1868.

The people finally got the chance to decide the courthouse issue thanks to an act ratified in the General Assembly on February 16, 1859. This piece of legislation ordered that the Harnett Sheriff hold an election on the first Thursday in April of 1859 to choose commissioners to locate a site for a new county seat to be called Lillington. The General Assembly was once again specific as to the county seat remaining within three miles of the geographic center of the county. Once the site was selected, another election was to be held at which the populace would decide between Toomer and Lillington.

The commissioners elected in the special April election included Anson Parker, Farquard Smith, Eldridge Stewart, R.C. Beldon, Stephen Pearson, John Elliott, and J.S. Harrington. The committee searched the woods of central Harnett until finally locating a site on a picturesque bluff overlooking the Cape Fear River This parcel of land on the edge of the 3-mile zone was owned by Nathaniel Jones, who gave the county an option on the desired 100 acres of land for $5 per acre.

In October of 1859, Elwood Morris, an engineer inspecting the works on the Cape Fear River, wrote Governor John W. Ellis the following observations about the upcoming election: "As Lillington is immediately upon an elevated Bank of the River, and commanding a view of it for several miles, its selection can hardly fail to please the friends of steamboat navigation on the Cape Fear."

The second special election of the year was held in Harnett on Thursday, October 27, 1859 to decide once and for all the issue between Toomer and Lillington. As was expected, the forces wanting to move the county seat to the bluff overlooking the Cape Fear prevailed, handily defeating Toomer's supporters. A breakdown of the vote was certified and submitted to Governor Ellis by Harnett Sherriff J.R. Grady. The results were as follows:

Averasboro	108	3
Grove	68	0
Neill's Creek	175	1
Buckhorn	83	30
Upper Little River	54	65
Barbecue	118	21
Stewart's Creek	18	20
Total	624	140

The justices moved quickly to build a courthouse on the new site as there were no facilities in Nathan Jones's woods to accommodate the courts even temporarily as there had been in Toomer. By early 1861, a wooden courthouse in Lillington was completed, and county courts began meeting there instead of Toomer.

5. War for Southern Independence

According to the 1860 Census, the first enumeration of the population since the creation of Harnett, the county was the home to 8,069 individuals, 30 percent of whom were listed as "non white." With approximately 1,600 men of military age, Harnett sent more than a thousand of her sons to fight for independence.

Historian Sion H. Harrington III made the following observations of Harnett's citizens on the eve of the war:

> They were poor people, mostly subsistence farmers who grew corn, sweet potatoes and peas, and raised hogs in order to feed their families. According to the 1860 Harnett County Agricultural Census, only 200 bales of cotton were raised in that year, and a mere 1,509 pounds of tobacco. Harnett was not a rich county. The very idea that poor men would leave their homes and families to die by the hundreds of disease or on some far away battlefield to protect the property of the rich, property they knew they would never own, is ludicrous.

Secession

The event that precipitated the War between the States was the success of abolitionists in electing their candidate on the Republican ticket as President of the United States. Abraham Lincoln won the race because the Democrats ran three candidates for the office, thus splitting their vote. Contrary to popular myth, Lincoln was not the popular choice, and won with only 40 percent of the vote. Lincoln did not receive a single vote in Harnett County. Locally, the votes in the crucial presidential election of 1860 broke down as follows: John C. Breckinridge, 542; John Bell, 138; and Stephen Douglas, 78.

Despite their disappointment at the outcome of the election, most North Carolinians did not feel that it was cause to leave the Union. Many were disturbed to see their cousins in states to the south break away but remained determined to stay a part of the United States as long as possible. Lincoln made this virtually impossible by calling on Governor John Ellis to raise troops to crush the secessionists in South Carolina and other Southern states. Before this call for

Second Lieutenant Jake Williams of Company C, 31st North Carolina Regiment, posed for this portrait during the Civil War. (Courtesy Wanda Gregory.)

troops, North Carolinians had assembled in a convention and rejected the proposal of leaving the Union. After the call for troops, Governor Ellis called for another convention, at which point the state exercised its Constitutional right to leave the Union on May 20, 1861.

Harnett was represented at the secession conventions by Colonel A.S. McNeill, who kept a low profile. There is no indication in the records of the proceedings that Colonel McNeill ever gave a speech either for or against the matter.

MILITARY UNITS FROM HARNETT

During the War Between the States, men from Harnett served the Confederate cause in military units throughout the South. Several units made up of men from Harnett were organized in the county and were later mustered into service as companies in regiments raised throughout the state. As the war progressed, individuals would volunteer or be drafted and often be assigned to serve in companies that had originally been organized in some other county. Hence, you might find individuals from Harnett serving in companies raised in counties from other areas of the state.

There were seven units that were raised predominantly in Harnett County. These saw action in battles in virtually every theatre of operation during the conflict. Most, however, served with General Robert E. Lee's Army of Northern Virginia.

The first company raised in Harnett was the Harnett Light Infantry, organized at Summerville on May 18, 1861. They were combined with other companies from across the state and became Company F, 5th North Carolina Volunteers. When the state reorganized its military units, the 5th North Carolina Volunteers became the 15th North Carolina Regiment. This unit engaged in some of the heaviest fighting of the war and was present at such battles as the Seven Days, Sharpsburg, Fredricksburg, the Wilderness, and Spotsylvania Courthouse. At the end of the war, only 138 men were present from the company when they were paroled on April 12, 1865.

The next company raised in Harnett was known as the Chalybeate Guards. They were officially designated as Company I, 31st North Carolina Regiment. This company was raised in the Chalybeate Springs area and mustered into service on October 30, 1861. It is interesting to note that C.H. Coffield, the man who introduced the measure creating the county, served as a first lieutenant in this company from October 30, 1861 until September 15, 1862.

The early history of the Chalybeate Guards is brief. Nearly the entire unit was captured when Roanoke Island fell in February of 1862. Upon reorganization, the unit participated in several notable engagements, including the fierce fighting in the defense of Petersburg, Virginia in 1864. They took part in the attack on Fort Harrison, Virginia, and as a result of the heavy fighting the 31st was decimated. Reports indicate that on September 30, 1864, a first lieutenant commanded the regiment, which could boast of only 60 men present for duty. What was left of the unit was sent to North Carolina to join General Joseph Johnston's army fighting against Sherman and surrendered with him in May of 1865.

The next unit from Harnett was enlisted at the courthouse in Lillington in March of 1862. They were mustered into state service in Raleigh on April 21, 1862, and became Company H, 50th North Carolina Regiment. Their training period was brief, and the unit was rushed north to Virginia to take part in the Seven Days battles. However, most of their fighting was done in North Carolina in such battles as New Bern and Washington. The 50th was one of the local units that participated in the battles of Averasboro and Bentonville in March of 1865. They were paroled at Greensboro on May 2, 1865.

A cavalry company known as the Highland Rangers was the next military unit to be organized in Harnett. They were organized at Summerville in April of 1862, and mustered into service at Goldsboro on April 28, 1862, with Captain Alexander Murchison serving as captain. This unit became Company D, 3rd North Carolina Cavalry, also known as the 41st North Carolina Regiment. The Highland Rangers primarily guarded wagon trains and patrolled eastern North Carolina and southeastern Virginia. In the spring of 1864, they moved north to become part of General Jeb Stuart's cavalry and saw much action under this noted commander. The unit participated in General Wade Hampton's Beef Steak Raid in September of 1864. In April of 1865, while shielding Lee's retreat from Petersburg, the Highland Rangers partook of the cavalry attacks that attempted to buy time for Lee's army to escape and were virtually annihilated. Few of those who survived agreed to surrender with the rest of Lee's army and stealthily escaped the Union army to fight another day.

An artillery regiment made up of Harnett County men was organized in Salisbury on May 9, 1862. Known as the Black River Tigers, they were officially designated as Company B, 10th Battalion, North Carolina Heavy Artillery, and their captain was Henry Barnes, who lived in the northeastern part of the county. The Black River Tigers spent most of the war manning the defenses of Fort Fisher, at the mouth of the Cape Fear River. In the fall of 1864, they were transferred to Georgia to help fight General William T. Sherman's army marching against Savannah. They participated in the fighting against Sherman for the remainder of the war, staying one step ahead of the Union army as they advanced north from Savannah through South Carolina and into North Carolina. They were one of the local units that participated in the battles at Averasboro and Bentonville in March of 1865, and surrendered with the rest of General Johnston's army at Greensboro on April 26, 1865.

As the war progressed, the Confederates found it necessary to create units that were made up of individuals who, under normal circumstances, would have been considered either too old or too young to participate. Two such units were created in Harnett.

Organized at Summerville in August of 1864, Company E, 78th North Carolina Regiment (8th Senior Reserves) was made up of some of the older men in the county. Their main action during the war was guarding the Wilmington &

Weldon Railroad and providing guards for prisoners. They were present at Fort Fisher during the first attack on December 24, 1864, and later were moved to Wilmington to man the defensive works around that city after Fort Fisher fell in January of 1865. Many of the members were present during the Battle of Averasboro and Bentonville, but the unit's records covering this period were lost so there are no specifics about their activities.

The younger men of Harnett were organized into a military unit known as Company H, 72nd North Carolina Regiment (3rd Junior Reserves). They were organized under Captain D.S. Byrd on January 3, 1865, and saw their first action in the Battle of Southwest Creek near Kinston on March 6–9, 1865. They also took part in the Battle of Bentonville. During Johnston's retreat across North

This is a portrait of Private George Wash Williams of Company C, 31st North Carolina Regiment (Courtesy Wanda Gregory.)

Chicora Cemetery is on the Averasboro battlefield.

Carolina, the unit lost many soldiers while fording the rain-swollen Haw River on April 15, 1865. The unit surrendered with the rest of Johnston's army.

BUCKHORN IRON WORKS

The iron operations at Buckhorn were at their peak during the War Between the States, and were an important source of iron for the workers in the Fayetteville Arsenal.

Because of the iron's importance, the locks and dams in the Cape Fear from Battle's Lock and Dam upstream were kept in good repair, as pig iron produced at Buckhorn was floated upstream by barge to Egypt in what is today Lee County. There it was placed on a train and taken along the Western Railroad to Fayetteville.

William McClane, a prominent individual in the development of the natural resources of central North Carolina, discovered the large iron ore deposit on the north bank of the Cape Fear River near Parker's Creek in Harnett County in

1858. Word of his discovery spread far and wide, and many scientists and geologists came to investigate the site.

The Buckhorn Iron Company was chartered later that year by the General Assembly. Their purpose was to produce iron from the ore deposits, which subsequent investigation had shown to be scattered across the Buckhorn Hills of northern Harnett. Many mines were opened in the region. The most prominent of these, the Buckhorn Mine, was located on Ore Hill about a mile downstream from Parker's Creek, while nearby were the Pegram Mine and the Dewar Mine. Across the river from the Buckhorn Mine was the Douglas Mine.

John Colvin was the ironmaster employed at Buckhorn. At Ore Hill he constructed an ingenious gravity-propelled tramway system to get ore from the top of the hill down to the barges on the river. The car at the top was loaded with ore and then released. A cable connected the loaded car with an empty one at the bottom. As the heavier car moved downhill, it pulled the lighter, empty one up the hill, where it was loaded and the process repeated.

Colvin also constructed a "log pen furnace." This type of furnace was built on the same principal as a normal blast furnace, but a log structure resembling the walls of a log cabin was built around the rock furnace and the intervening space filled with earth. This type of furnace was used to add an extra bit of stability to the large rock walls. Colvin's furnace was called "Ock Nock," which, according to historian Malcolm Fowler, meant "rock pot." Fowler also reported a legend that maintained that Colvin made an extremely high grade of iron from his furnace after one of his workers "slid down the charging chute into its roaring maw and vanished with a blood chilling scream in a puff of smoke."

The Buckhorn Iron operations remained in operation until virtually the very end of the war, when they were destroyed by Yankee soldiers. Charles B. Mallett of Wilmington, half owner of the works, wrote in 1865, "The Ocknock Iron Works on Buckhorn Falls, capable of making 80 tons of Iron per month & 1/2 interest of C.B. Mallett was burned ($20,000 loss) by Gen. Sherman's Army."

BUSHWACKERS AND MARAUDERS

The remote character of portions of the western half of Harnett made it a good place for deserters and ruffians from across central North Carolina to take refuge. The thick forests and swamps along Anderson Creek and the woods west of Raven Rock became the haunt of many of these lawless characters.

Unfortunately, these individuals were not content with merely hiding out until the war was over. Instead, many of them used the opportunity of the absence of the men of the community to prey upon the virtually defenseless women and children.

In November of 1863, a band of these ruffians masquerading as members of the 56th North Carolina Regiment fell upon a house in Harnett. In a letter to Lieutenant Colonel Kenneth Murchison, commanding the 24th Battalion of the Home Guard, the adjutant general noted that the raiders had "removed a woman

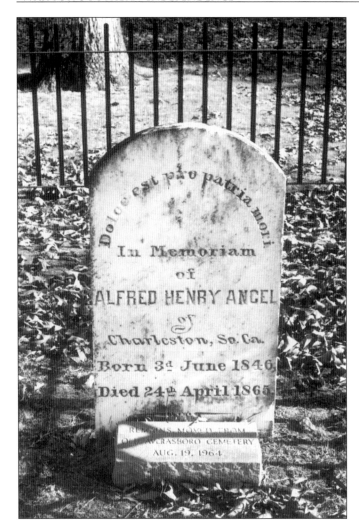

This is the final resting place of Alfred Angel of Charleston, South Carolina, who was mortally wounded during the battle of Averasboro.

and child from it, and set fire to and burnt up house." He instructed Murchison to hunt down the party and bring them to justice.

In the summer of 1864, Home Guard units in the area descended on Moore, Randolph, and Montgomery Counties to clear out the hotbed of deserters who had become so bold and numerous that on two occasions they threatened to descend on Carthage and burn the place to the ground.

By August 5, 1864, the unit had rounded up a good number of prisoners at the Moore County seat, from which point the troops set out for the Western Railroad depot at Spout Springs, where the prisoners were to be placed on the train and taken to Fayetteville. Before they could reach their destination, the column was ambushed and a spirited skirmish ensued. In the melee, three of the Confederates were killed, as well as an unrecorded number of the bushwackers. Two of the prisoners managed to escape in the confusion.

The bodies of the three Confederate dead were taken back to Carthage and put on public display.

The Confederates did manage to capture a prisoner, William S. Cockman, who was found sitting against a tree with an empty gun in his hand. Though there was no concrete evidence that he had fired the weapon and killed anyone, he was found guilty of being an accessory to the crime and sentenced to hang. He appealed his case to the North Carolina Supreme Court, but the sentence was upheld. Before he could be executed, Cockman was liberated from the Moore County jail, apparently by some of his fellow desperadoes.

In October of 1864, the adjutant general issued orders to Captain J.W. McLeod, commander of Company B of the Home Guard in Harnett, to move into the northwestern portion of the county where a band of deserters were "committing depredations." As a sign of how formidable some of these bands of outlaws could be, McLeod was instructed as follows: "if you have too few men, call on the nearest HG captain to aid you."

THE YANKEES DESCEND ON HARNETT

In March of 1865, the Union army under General William T. Sherman reached Fayetteville following a march that had taken them from Savannah, Georgia, to Columbia, South Carolina, and on into North Carolina. A path of destruction followed in his wake.

Leaving Fayetteville, several factors compelled Sherman to divide his army into two wings. One of the main factors was the horrible condition of the roads, which had been soaked by the nearly constant rains that had fallen during the winter of 1865. Unbeknownst to the Confederates, he was heading to Goldsboro to link up with other Union forces operating in eastern North Carolina. As he crossed the Cape Fear, his right wing struck out via central Sampson County. His left wing followed the Fayetteville and Northern Plank Road towards Averasboro.

Confederate General Joseph E. Johnston ordered Lieutenant General William J. Hardee to impede Sherman's left wing in an effort to ascertain Sherman's true destination, as well as to create distance between the wings of Sherman's army. To accomplish this, Hardee placed his corps in position across a narrow strip of land between the Cape Fear and Black River on the Cumberland/Harnett line. An intense battle followed, which cost more than a thousand men their lives. Known as the Battle of Averasboro, Hardee's outnumbered men held their position through a rainy March 16, 1865, checking the advance of the Union Army for a full day and buying time for Johnston to assemble his scattered forces to strike a blow at one wing of Sherman's army. The Confederates successfully carried out all of their objectives, then withdrew during the night to rejoin the main body of Johnston's army in Johnston County.

Many of the private homes in the vicinity of the battle were used to house wounded soldiers. The most notable of these in Harnett was the Lebanon Plantation, which was used as a hospital during and immediately after the battle.

This marker is for the remains of Confederate soldiers killed in Averasboro.

Other houses in the county that took in the wounded from the battle included the Neill Stewart home, which once stood near Erwin; the William Avera home; and the Dushee Shaw Half-Way House.

After the battle, as the Union army crossed Black River and continued its march east towards Goldsboro, foraging parties and cavalry screens were thrown out across southeastern Harnett as the army passed through. A month later, Sherman's army was back in Harnett, having traveled there via Goldsboro and Raleigh. Contingents of his army were encamped along the Cape Fear in Chatham and had fanned out as far downstream as the Buckhorn Iron Works. They were preparing to cross the river in pursuit of the Confederates when Johnston surrendered his army at the Bennett Place near Durham.

Other contingents of the Union army had traversed Harnett west of the Cape Fear while Sherman was marching with his main force across the eastern part of the county. Cavalry in quest of the trains carrying the machinery from the Fayetteville Arsenal made it as far as the Spout Springs area before breaking off pursuit. There is also a note in a Raleigh paper stating that the Yankees burned Summerville.

Another force of Union cavalry moved up the road from Fayetteville towards McNeill's Ferry and Lillington. Tradition maintains that this group continued upstream and crossed the river on a pontoon bridge they constructed at Northington's Ferry before rejoining Sherman's army. No official record of the bridge survived the war, but they apparently left the bridge behind, for it remained in place for several years, showing up on at least one map of the era as a prominent landmark in Harnett County.

6. THE LEAN YEARS

The county and her citizens were in bad shape following the unsuccessful conclusion of the war. Not only were many of her sons killed or maimed in the fighting, but the county had been host to two armies that foraged within her borders during the latter days of the war. Then came the heavy hand of the Federal occupation forces who united with individuals of questionable character to take advantage of the recently freed slaves and exploit the downtrodden condition of the people.

Many individuals picked up and moved west, following a trail blazed earlier when hard financial times caused many citizens to move along in search of new opportunities. Others decided to stay home and make the most of a difficult situation. Stripped of their right to rule themselves, several of the former Confederates joined vigilante bands to restore order from the chaos. Thus, the Ku Klux Klan came to Harnett.

Contrary to popular myth, the Klan did not evolve as an organization to terrorize African Americans. Instead, their targets were mostly those who aided the Federal occupation forces, regardless of race. Oftentimes targets of their violence were white members of the community, guilty of some crime or offense. The "supernatural" image of the Klan riders came from the ghostly dress and ghoulish masks they wore. In its early days, most members were animated by a sense of fighting to restore self rule.

The Klan was especially strong in the Averasboro area. In an effort to break up the group, Federal authorities infiltrated their ranks with an informant. His purpose and identity soon discovered, the man was gunned down in the street by an unknown assailant as Federal marshals were riding into town to pick up a membership list he had compiled. This led to a mass exodus from the town, and Averasboro's population dwindled to a point from which it would never recover. Soon after this incident, the Federal occupation ended, and home rule was restored. The Klan had outlived its purpose, and soon ceased to exist on a large scale.

In 1873, the General Assembly passed "An Act to Incorporate the Town of Averasboro, In the County of Harnett." Several old towns throughout the state were "reincorporated" in the days of Reconstruction so that their operations would conform to the new system of government imposed upon the state by the Federal government. Under this new law, Averasboro's boundaries were delineated and officers were named. Neill Stewart, W.S. Rhodes, and Thomas Fowler were made commissioners; H.C. Avera was mayor; and Rat Clements became constable.

Dr. John McCormick was a prominent Harnett resident during and after the Civil War.

While Averasboro was in a state of decline, Lillington was beginning to grow, albeit slowly at first. On April 3, 1866, the sale of lots within the town was advertised in the Fayetteville newspapers. The sale was scheduled to take place on May 18, 1866, and the commissioners appointed to handle the sale offered terms "on a credit of nine months." Commissioners for this sale included John McCormick, James S. Harrington, A.S. McNeill, James M. Turner, and John Green.

On February 8, 1872, the county seat was officially incorporated as a town. The act delineated the town's boundaries, set up its government structure, and provided for election of a mayor, three commissioners, and a constable. It also stated that the county officials could not grant a liquor license to an individual without the prior approval of the town commissioners.

That same year, the first attempt to construct a bridge at Lillington was launched. The Lillington Bridge Company was incorporated and given a 30-year monopoly to build and operate a bridge over the river, but they were not successful. The only bridge they are known to have constructed was erected *c.* 1874, but was destroyed by a freshet before it was completed. Visitors to the county seat from the east side of the river still found it necessary to cross the Cape Fear at Lillington via Purefoy's Ferry until the early days of the twentieth century.

COUNTY'S FINANCIAL WOES

Harnett's finances took a long time to recover from the war. The county came into being on the eve of the war and was the object of several lawsuits already discussed. The loss of the war and the chaos that followed made matters worse.

Since 1855, the county's prisoners had been housed in the Cumberland jail thanks to the fiasco surrounding Harnett's first attempt at jail construction. But by 1867, Cumberland informed Harnett that the latter would have to look after their own prisoners. This was quite a problem for the county, as Harnett had no money with which to undertake new construction projects. County officials built a log jail in the most economical fashion they could. The finished product was a four-room building with holes cut into the walls for ventilation and light. This structure stood just north of the courthouse and served Harnett for over 30 years.

Historian D.P. McDonald recalled the hard financial times Harnett County faced in the years following the War between the States.

> Money was scarce and taxes hard to collect after the war. There were no banks nearer than Raleigh and Fayetteville. The Treasurer carried the money in his pocket, or kept it at home in a trunk. When Rora Barnes was Treasurer in 1868-70 he kept it in a drawer in his store in Lillington. With a revenue of seven or eight thousand a year, the Commissioners had to meet a demand for twelve or fourteen thousand annually. County orders were issued on the Treasurer for payment of the debts and he had no funds to meet them. Credit was zero . . . The 'county script' as the

county orders were then called, were of little more value than the Confederate money that was kept with the hope that it would sometime be redeemed at some price.

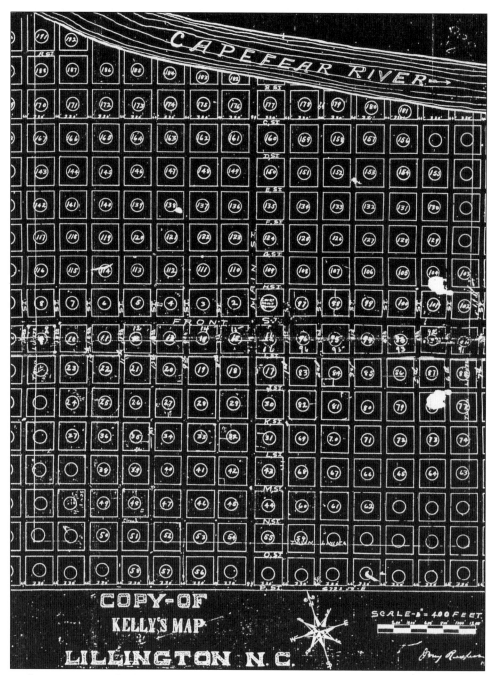

Kelly's 1907 map of Lillington shows the town's situation on the Cape Fear River.

One enterprising fellow from Fayetteville, Henry Lilly, came through the area buying up the county script for a fraction of its face value. Once he had collected more than $25,000 worth of the notes, he took the county to court to collect the debt. The commissioners compromised and agreed to pay $13,000, which Lilly accepted. But when the commissioners put the matter of a special tax to pay the debt on the ballot, voters turned it down. Thus the "Lilly Debt" remained unpaid and the county's credit went from bad to worse.

With such financial problems, the county could not afford for their sheriff to be merciful in his tax collecting duties. They needed a sheriff who would get tough with folks and bring in as much money as possible. They found that Sheriff Kenneth McNeill was the wrong man for this task.

In 1872, Harnett citizens had elected Kenneth McNeill to serve as sheriff. McNeill was a man noted for his kindness and was well-liked by the people, but these qualities made it virtually impossible to carry out one of the main duties of a sheriff in those days—tax collecting.

McNeill could not bear to extract taxes from many of his fellow citizens who were eking out a meager existence. County commissioners wanted McNeill to get tough and extract as much money as was possible from the poor farmers of Harnett, but he didn't have the heart to turn people out of their homes so their property could be auctioned off for delinquent taxes. He collected what he could but refused to come down hard on folks.

Finally, county treasurer C.H. Coffield brought suit against Sheriff McNeill for the amount of unpaid taxes for the year 1874. McNeill refused to come up with the money and took his case all the way to the North Carolina Supreme Court. He was successful and thus avoided the undesirable penalty of paying the tax bill himself. But he was thoroughly disgusted with the job and the way the commissioners were acting, so he resigned from office shortly thereafter.

To fill the vacancy, the commissioners appointed John A. Green. Historian Malcolm Fowler preserved the following rhyme, which the noted balladeer George W. Miller penned for the occasion:

> Whoever knew such treatment as this the sheriff has received?
> But since he is out of office, he is very much relieved.
> He's not bothered with the tax list now, and nothing of the sort,
> For it's been assigned to John A. Green and he will make it snort.

Despite having the unenviable task of increasing the tax collection, Green was a successful and well-liked sheriff. The records of the county for this era are sparse, so there are few details of his service. Green found out early just how bad off the county was financially. According to Allan Shaw, Sheriff Green had to borrow money from a friend to pay the jurors at the first court session he attended after his election. But he managed to hold the office for a dozen years and was known affectionately as Sheriff Green for the rest of his days, despite attaining higher office.

BUCKHORN IRON OPERATIONS

George G. Lobdell of the Lobdell Car Wheel Company obtained a wheel from a Confederate train, and the iron wheel stood up to the tests his engineers devised better than any wheel his company produced. He thereafter set about on a search that eventually led him from his home in Delaware to central North Carolina.

Lobdell was one of the principals behind the founding of the Cape Fear Iron and Steel Company, which acquired the various iron works along the Deep and Cape Fear Rivers.

Upon finding that the best grade of iron was produced from the Buckhorn mines in Harnett, the company obtained mining rights in a lease from owner A.J. DeRosset of Wilmington.

Upon further examination, Lobdell found the Buckhorn iron to be of extremely high quality. At the site of Colvin's old furnace, Lobdell constructed what State Geologist Jasper Stuckey described as "the first modern blast furnace erected in North Carolina."

This was a hot blast furnace standing 54 feet tall with "10 feet diameter of bosh." A screw turbine to power the machinery and operate the bellows was mounted in a dam built across the old canal constructed nearly 75 years before to bypass Buckhorn Falls.

The furnace at Buckhorn remained in blast only about three months, then fell silent. Iron from the Buckhorn Mine and those in the surrounding hills was transported upstream to be worked at the Endor Furnace. The reason the Buckhorn Furnace stopped has remained a mystery and probably had more to do with mechanical failure or the financial problems of the 1870s than a lack of ore. Iron operations in the area wound to a close by the 1880s, at which point Lobdell returned to Delaware.

The Buckhorn Furnace remained in place as late as 1893, when H.B.T. Nitze wrote, "Although the furnace has been idle ever since, and most of the woodwork, outbuildings, etc., are decayed and in ruins, the stack itself has been kept in fair repair, and might well be moved to some regular ore supply and made a paying investment."

JEFFERSON COUNTY

On January 8, 1887, Dr. John McCormick of Harnett County and Isaac Bailey of Mitchell County introduced a bill in the State Senate to create a new county to be known as Jefferson, which would have been carved from parts of Harnett, Moore, and Chatham Counties.

In essence, it would have included the land now belonging to Lee County, plus the western third of Harnett. The issue was hotly debated, with proponents equally vocal on both sides. Many petitions were circulated through the affected area, and in the end the forces against creating a new county carried the day.

WILSON SHORTCUT RAILROAD
AND THE FOUNDING OF DUNN

There were some bright spots for the county in all of the financial gloom, as one of the county's most important transportation arteries was constructed during this period. This railroad actually had its beginnings in the 1830s when a railroad was proposed to connect Raleigh and Wilmington.

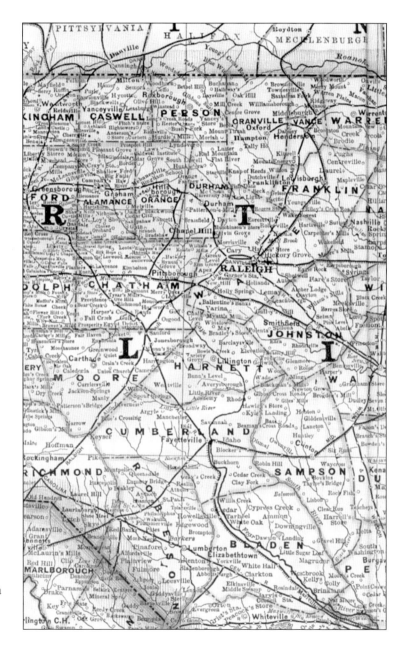

This section of Cram's 1885 New Railroad and County Map of North Carolina and South Carolina shows Harnett County.

These plans never materialized, but the company did manage to connect the port city with Weldon. Changing their name to reflect this, the Wilmington and Weldon Railroad became an important thoroughfare across the state and served as a vital supply line for the Confederate forces in Virginia during the War Between the States. After the war, the railroad provided an important link for trains headed up the eastern seaboard. Their line took a circuitous route across the state however, going from Florence, South Carolina to Wilmington, then north to Weldon. To shorten the trip, the company decided in the summer of 1885 to construct a rail along a new route known as the "Wilson Short Cut." This line left Wilson and traveled south to Florence via Fayetteville, saving 60 miles.

Workers began construction in Wilson and by October of 1886 had reached Fayetteville. The line cut across Harnett east of Black River and was built on a swath of land received from Henry and Eliza Pope. Though the final link in the "Wilson Short Cut" was not completed to Florence until February of 1892, the rail lines provided an important outlet for people in the region through which it passed. This was especially true of those individuals in the relatively remote portion of Harnett.

The first lots for a new town along this railroad were auctioned from a caboose on October 26, 1886, and the new town was known as Dunn, named in honor of Captain Bennett R. Dunn, an engineer for the railroad. Originally laid out in a circular fashion, the town was officially incorporated on February 12, 1887, and quickly grew into the commercial hub of a four-county region that included eastern Harnett, northeastern Cumberland, northwestern Sampson, and southwestern Johnston. The infant town quickly surpassed Averasboro and Lillington as Harnett's largest town.

But for all its commercial promise, Dunn was a rough place. Long before the railroad came through, the community thereabouts was known as Tearshirt, in honor of a tavern in the area in which was displayed a torn shirt, a souvenir from some memorable brawl. The "duel" nature of Dunn was noted in an article in the May 30, 1889 issue of the *Fayetteville Observer Weekly*:

> There are few towns in the State whose progress is more rapid and substantial than Dunn's. Several new buildings are in course of erection, among which are two new hotels and a large brick store. A splendid trade in the fall is anticipated by all merchants.
>
> A most disgraceful riot occurred in Dunn on Saturday evening late. Knives, clubs and sticks were indifferently handled, but no serious damage was done. The warrant issued for the arrest of the peace breakers contained a list of names which, if written in a line, would measure probably ten feet in length.

The rise of Dunn sealed the doom of Harnett's great inland port city at Averasboro. Many of the people who remained hoped that the railroad would pass through the old town.

When it went just a few miles to the east, they packed up and moved to the railroad, some even disassembling their houses and rebuilding them in Dunn. The final blow to the old town came when the Masonic Lodge, Palmyra 187, moved to Dunn in 1888.

STRUGGLES OVER THE COURTHOUSE LOCATION

By the 1880s, the wooden courthouse in Lillington was beginning to show signs of wear, but with the county's financial situation, there was little chance of raising enough money to effect the necessary repairs. Thus, problems that were at first minor went unremedied and grew into larger problems.

On March 2, 1887, an act was passed by the General Assembly calling for the commissioners of the county to levy a special tax for the year 1887 not to exceed "ten cents on every hundred dollars' worth of property and thirty cents on each poll." The tax could not be levied, however, without a vote of the people. The thrifty Scots of Harnett decided that the courthouse repairs did not warrant a new tax, and the measure was defeated.

The General Assembly ratified an act on March 11, 1889 that called for a special election to be held in Harnett. The purpose was to decide whether or not to remove the courthouse from Lillington and make the bustling young town of Dunn the county seat. Expenses for this special election were to be paid by the people in Averasboro Township.

This photograph shows Dunn's Broad Street in 1898.

Furthermore, the law specified that if the proponents of the move were successful, construction of the new edifices of county government was to be paid by "private subscription" and not by special tax levy or from the county's general fund.

On April 1, 1889, a group of citizens concerned about the removal of the county seat gathered in the courthouse in Lillington. J.P. Hodges was named chairman of the meeting, and T.W. Harrington secretary. Soon, several individuals came forward to make speeches against the proposed move. These included some of the county's most noteworthy citizens of the time, including Colonel John A. Spears, Dr. John McCormick, Thomas A. Harrington, and William Pearson, the latter being Harnett's lone representative in the General Assembly. *The State Chronicle* noted, "The speeches were all forcible and to the point, and well received by the audience, as evidenced by the rounds of applause."

Following the speeches, a series of resolutions was brought before the meeting by Harrington, Spears, and Daniel Green. All the resolutions were adopted unanimously. Later they were published and spread across the county. The resolutions were as follows:

> RESOLVED, That it is the sense of this meeting that even if a removal of the county site from Lillington, under the present act, be lawful and constitutional, still we believe it would be oppressive and unduly burdensome on a great majority of our fellow citizens.
>
> RESOLVED, That, whilst we have not time to enlarge on all the objections to the removal proposed, we say that the proposition to

The Cam Rob Strickland family is shown here in front of their home near Averasboro in 1898.

remove a county site from the centre of a county to an edge of the same is always objectionable for obvious reasons.

RESOLVED, That in this case, if removal should take place, many of our citizens, not only at court time but at all times, when necessary to visit the court house, would have to travel 30 to 45 miles and to cross Cape Fear river. At Lillington it is only about one fourth of a mile from said river where there is a free ferry. The nearest point to Dunn on said river is about four miles.

RESOLVED, That we seriously doubt the obligation of the township of Averasboro to pay the expenses of the election in this question, and we note in the act that no specifications are even alluded to as to the quality of the public buildings proposed to be built, and as such building is proposed to be gratuitous we fear it would not be done, even if necessary.

RESOLVED, That we now have a suitable court house and jail, and that the charge publicly made that the court house is "nearly rotten down" is not true.

RESOLVED, "That the proceedings of this meeting be sent to the *State Chronicle* for publication, with request that the *Harnett Courier, Fayetteville Observer* and *Goldsboro Messenger* copy the same.

The supporters of removing the county seat to Dunn responded to this circular. In the May 1, 1889 issue of the *Courier* they expressed their views with the following statement:

The question of Removal is one of importance to the whole county and as most of our readers, we suppose, have seen the paper referred to above, we will submit a few reasons on the other side of the question. If the assertions of one of the boldest champions of the opposition are true no one will be compelled to make this three days journey of 47 miles, or even 40, and if it is 47 miles to the most remote corner of the county, there are but few people within the bounds of Harnett that live more than 35 miles from Dunn and not many that are even that far.

We admit that the present situation of the county site is one convenient to a few who have nearly all the conveniences Harnett County has ever given anyone. We say the county seat should be moved.

1st. Because Dunn is the commercial center of the county, and that it is more convenient to the majority of the people who have business at court, and with the county officers.

2nd. Lillington is a place with no future, and Dunn is a live town with bright prospects. The Removal of the county seat will give an additional impetus to the growth of the town and help it to become a better home market for all kinds of country produce.

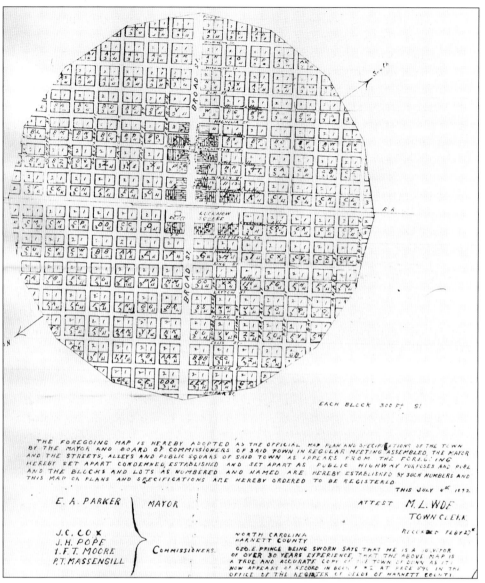

This 1892 map of Dunn was taken from the original survey.

3rd. The Removal means a bridge across Cape Fear River beyond the least shadow of a doubt, notwithstanding all that the opposition may say to the contrary, and with the county site and a bridge across the river, Dunn will naturally become a place of importance, and the taxes upon the increased valuation of property in this section of the county will soon save our good western brethren more than enough in their taxes to pay for the extra trouble of coming to Dunn, even if they have to attend court here, "for half a century to come."

4th. The same energy and perseverance that put the Removal Bill through the last Legislature, can put a New County Bill through.

5th. The present Court House and Jail are NOT suitable buildings, and any man that has any county pride ought to be ashamed of them. The county is insolvent, and the voters refused to vote a special tax to make repairs after the commissioners had been indicted on account of the condition of the Court House. You now have the offer of a court house and jail for nothing. The opposition tells you that, in all probability you will be offered a worthless shanty. The commissioners cannot be made to move the county seat to Dunn until suitable buildings are provided, by private subscription.

It does seem to us that if the voters of Harnett do not vote for the removal, they will lose a great opportunity for advancing the interests of the WHOLE COUNTY.

With the battle lines thus drawn, the proponents for each side began the task of convincing their neighbors to vote for their side of the issue. Speeches were held in communities all across the county. A writer in the *Fayetteville Observer* on May 9, 1889 noted, "The campaign in Harnett on the question of removing the county seat from Lillington to Dunn is waxing pretty warm. Speech making commenced last Monday and will end at Dunn next Monday. Both sides are hopeful of victory."

On May 6, 1889, L.J. Best, I.A. Murchison, J.R. Godwin, and C.I. Stewart, proponents in favor of the measure, set out from Dunn to "canvass Harnett County." Small crowds usually greeted them at most locales, but at Lillington they were met by a large group of citizens. When they had finished their speeches, Colonel J.A. Spears and former sheriff John A. Green came to the rostrum and argued for keeping the county seat in Lillington.

On May 14, 1889, the election was held. Supporters for keeping the county seat near the center of the county at Lillington won the day. Unfortunately, the totals of the votes have not been preserved. Thus was born the bitter rivalry between Dunn and Lillington.

COURTHOUSE FIRE OF 1892

On Saturday, October 15, 1892, the old wooden courthouse in Lillington was destroyed by fire. The fire broke out in the wee hours of the morning and destroyed many records of the clerk of court, the register of deeds, and the county's tax books.

The cause of the fire was never discovered, but an arsonist was at work in town at the time. A correspondent for the *Carthage Blade* noted, "There appears to be something remarkable about the town of Lillington, as only a few nights ago S.A. Salmon's store and stock were burned. The fire fiend seems to be putting in some of his heaviest blows."

Another blow befell the county a couple of weeks later when County Treasurer Allen Byrd was robbed. A thief broke into his house and absconded with the trunk containing the county's funds, which on this occasion amounted to $800. As the editor of the *Central Times* opined, "The Court House burned and the Treasurer robbed leaves us in a bad row of stumps to run county affairs." Byrd worked hard to make up for the loss, and paid back all but $363.30, which was forgiven by a special act of the legislature passed on March 6, 1895.

COURTHOUSE TO TURLINGTON'S CROSSROADS

Through the winter of 1893, petitions were circulating through the county once again to remove the county seat from Lillington. This time, the strongest contender was Turlington's Crossroads, the intersection of the old Lillington to Dunn Road and the Stage Road.

The firm of Taylor and Slocumb, which ran a mercantile operation at the crossroads and was heavily involved in the naval stores business in the area, offered to give the county 5 acres of land to erect a new courthouse and jail. Furthermore, they pledged $1,000 toward the construction of the county's buildings with brick.

There were many individuals, mostly staunch advocates of Dunn or Lillington, who did not take the offer seriously. But in a letter to the editor of the *Central Times* dated February 23, 1893, a writer from Turlington's Crossroads pointed out the advantages of the site. "Some burlesques and some sarcasm has been cast at the Court House offer at the X Roads at Turlington's by Taylor and Slocumb. But here are the various distances to the county line on all sides. South 7 miles, North 11 miles, East 9 miles, West 26 miles; and about 4 miles from Averasboro Ferry , and 5 miles from McNeill's Ferry, which is the best one in the county."

The site would have been centrally located in the county when the western townships of Johnsonville and Upper Little River were severed, as most thought would eventually happen despite the failure to create the county of Jefferson with Sanford as county seat five years earlier.

But the proponents for the new site were not able to muster enough support from the Dunn folks to overcome the Lillington group, and the effort failed. Advocates for moving the courthouse to Dunn continued their efforts for the next four years.

TEMPORARY COURTHOUSES

Shortly after the fire of 1892, county officials made arrangements to rent space for a courtroom, register of deeds office, and clerk of court's office from Ben Rich, who operated a tavern across the street from the old courthouse. Rich's saloon was renowned for being able to supply the large quantities of whiskey needed to slake the thirst of Harnett citizens who gathered when Superior Court was in session, as well as on election night.

Whether or not Rich continued operating his barroom after the fall of 1892 is uncertain. If he did, it must have been a very convenient and lucrative arrangement. Regardless, his saloon proved adequate for the transacting of government affairs until the winter of 1894.

At 3:30 a.m. on Friday, February 9, 1894, fire destroyed Harnett's temporary courthouse. The *Central Times* reported the incident in their February 15, 1894 edition, which stated, "The fire originated in the second story of the building. The fire had made such progress before it was discovered that nothing in the second story was saved.

"All the trial papers being in the office, the records and books of the clerk that were not immediately connected with the trial docket (being on the first floor) were saved. . . . It is thought that the fire was accidental as the door to the stair case was found securely locked when the parties who first reached the fire arrived."

The fire left the county in dire straits as there were, at the time, no vacant buildings in Lillington large enough to house the county government. To alleviate this problem, Silas Salmon (who served as Harnett sheriff from 1898 to 1904) obtained an old wooden building at Summerville and had it moved to a vacant lot in Lillington.

County Commission records show that Salmon was paid $80 per year to cover rent for this building. The structure stood on the south side of Front Street near the present site of the Front Street Café. Despite its obvious deficiencies, the

This 1905 postcard shows Broad Street in Dunn, looking east.

ramshackle old building has the distinction of having been the site of one of the most famous trials in Harnett's history, that of Ed Purvis. On the railroad between Benson and Dunn, Purvis had killed W.J. Blackwell, a flagman on the train. Purvis was apprehended after a large manhunt, tried, and found guilty of murder. For his crime he received the death penalty and was executed on November 17, 1897.

Purvis's execution was a grand spectacle, as approximately 6,000 descended upon the county seat to watch the hanging. The event took place in what was then a wooded ravine but is now the parking lot behind the courthouse. Purvis's body was purchased for $5 by Dr. Ollen Lee Denning of Dunn, who used the cadaver to teach anatomy classes and later displayed the skeleton in his medical office.

This sketch of the execution of Ed Purvis was drawn by eyewitness Albert Harrell of Dunn.

7. POLITICAL TURMOIL AND PROSPERITY

By the year 1896, Harnett's finances were still in a bad state, and there seemed little hope of raising enough money to pay the county's debts, let alone embark on a much needed public buildings campaign. The old ramshackle building assembled by Silas Salmon still served as the county's courthouse. The idea of removing the county seat to Dunn resurfaced again, but with the bitter fight of 1889 still fresh in everyone's mind, the movement gained little momentum.

Sheriff John Green, ever the public-minded citizen, applied his active mind to the county's financial woes and soon worked out the idea of issuing bonds to raise enough money to pay off the county's debt. His calculations showed that if the bonds were issued and the old debt paid, there would still be enough money to build a new courthouse. It was a bold idea. So bold, in fact, that when he presented the idea at the Democrat Convention in Lillington in 1896, he was scoffed at and ridiculed for cooking up what many believed to be a risky scheme.

Not one to easily give up, Sheriff Green presented his plan the following week to a joint county convention of the Populists and Republicans. Their reaction was the exact opposite of the Democrats. Not only was the proposal heartily endorsed, Sheriff Green was placed on the "Fusion Ticket" for election as county commissioner. The Populists and Republicans had joined forces to throw out the moneyed interests of the Democrats, "fusing" their tickets, hence the term.

For the people of Harnett, the election of 1896 was one of the first elections since the War between the States in which they had a legitimate alternative to the Democratic Party. Prior to the war, many who lived in the area had been firm Whigs, but when that party dissolved on the eve of the war, many had no home. For the years following the war, very few openly professed to being Republicans. As historian Allen Shaw once noted, Harnett residents of this period were of an "Independent bent."

The Populists/Republicans carried the election of 1896 in Harnett, soundly defeating the Democrats. The ever popular Green was named chairman of the Board of Commissioners, and his plans to end the county's financial woes were put in motion.

COURTHOUSE BUILT

By the fall of 1897, the contract for the courthouse was let, and a brick kiln was set up on the outskirts of Lillington, just southeast of town. Work on the project was delayed when the kiln collapsed, destroying 20,000 bricks.

The cornerstone of the county's new brick courthouse was laid in the southeast corner by Mrs. W.J. Washburn of Lillington and Mrs. Mozella Perry of Franklinton on June 8, 1898.

Construction proceeded rapidly. Within two weeks, the walls were erected to the second floor. It is uncertain exactly when the structure was completed, but it was in use by the fall of 1898.

County commissioners had agreed in their July 1898 meeting to put up one-quarter of the amount necessary to erect a brick cupola on the courthouse, provided the rest of the proceeds could be raised from the public. County records do not record the exact price, but there were obviously sufficient funds for the construction of the cupola that was built on the front of the building and also for the bell that was installed in the belfry.

This photograph of the Harnett County courthouse in Lillington was taken in the early twentieth century. (Courtesy North Carolina Department of Archives and History.)

Dr. John Taylor Williams

One Republican who gained notoriety during this era was Dr. John Taylor Williams, who was appointed U.S. consul to Sierra Leone in 1897 by President William McKinley. Williams was born in 1859 to Peter and Flora Williams, free African Americans who lived in the pine forests of southwestern Harnett where Peter made a living in the naval stores and lumber business. Flora taught her son to read and nurtured his thirst for knowledge.

One story preserved about John Taylor Williams recalls the time he spent working the turpentine operations of his uncle near the present site of Benhaven School. The boy asked that fatback be taken from his daily meal rations and an extra amount of money put into his pay at the end of the week instead. When asked his reasons, Williams replied that he was saving his money to buy books.

By 1876, Williams had mastered his studies sufficiently to be admitted to the State Normal School in Fayetteville. He graduated at the top of his class in 1880. After a brief stint teaching school in places including Lillington, Southport, and Charlotte, Williams entered Leonard Medical College in Raleigh. He graduated from that institution in 1886, and became one of the first African Americans licensed by the North Carolina Board of Medical Examiners. He returned to Charlotte where he became a pillar of the community. In addition to being chief surgeon at Union Hospital, he was also a successful businessman and active member of the church.

Dr. John Taylor Williams resided in Charlotte the remainder of his life, returning periodically to Harnett to transact business. At some point around the turn of the century his former neighbors asked his uncle what had become of the studious nephew. After giving the matter some thought, he replied, "I don't know exactly, but hear tell he's took up preaching at a church called Liberia." He was referring, of course, to the fact that Williams was frequently in neighboring Liberia while consul to Sierra Leone, a post in which he served throughout the administrations of Presidents McKinley and Teddy Roosevelt.

Williams died on June 8, 1924, and is buried in Charlotte. A school in the "Queen City" still bears the noted Harnettian's name.

Democrats Regain Nominal Control

The Democratic elite were stunned by the successes of the Fusionists. Their initial defeats in 1894, followed by their total rejection by North Carolina voters in 1896, led to dark days for the party. One bright note was that they had been able to work out a deal with the Populists whereby both parties agreed to support Democratic Presidential candidate William Jennings Bryan, who subsequently carried the state with 20,000 votes over William McKinley.

To regain their lost power, the Democrats embarked on a vigorous campaign to oust the Fusionists. Their central theme was not philosophical or political debate. Instead, it was the question of race and the role African Americans should play in governing North Carolina. In their definitive work, *North Carolina: The History of a Southern State*, historians Hugh Lefler and A.R. Newsome made the following observations on the Democrats' comeback strategy:

> Under the shrewd leadership of State Chairman Furnifold M. Simmons, the Democrats resorted to unprecedented organization, correspondence, publicity, and stump speaking. The intimidation of Negro voters was a cardinal feature of Democratic strategy. They attacked the vulnerable record of the Fusionists and, recognizing the danger as well as the effectiveness of their strategy, they raised the issue of white supremacy and stirred the embers of racial hatred.

The strategy of racial division was successful in driving a wedge between the Populists and Republicans, especially in central and eastern North Carolina. The Republicans in North Carolina still carried the stigma of being associated with Lincoln and the radical abolitionists, and memories of the chaos and misrule of the dark days of Reconstruction were fresh in many people's minds. Remembering the lawlessness of the carpetbaggers and the Freedmen's Bureau, North Carolinians could easily believe reports coming out of the eastern part of the state of near anarchy occurring under the administration of the black leadership that had been able to vote itself into power with the Fusionists. Nearly all African Americans registered to vote in those days were registered Republican.

This photograph of the Dunn Progressive Institute was taken in February, 1902.

The Democrats' campaign strategy in Harnett County was masterminded by Dan Hugh McLean, known as the "Silver Tongued Orator of the Cape Fear" because of his skill in public speaking. McLean was chairman of the party in the initial stages of the campaign but later stepped down in order to accept a nomination to the General Assembly. This was a wise move on the Democrats' part, as McLean was popular with many folks in Harnett due to the fact that he had spent many years in service to his state. He enlisted in the Confederate Army at the age of 14 and was sent home because of his youth. He later enlisted in the North Carolina Junior Reserves. Many people referred to him with the honorary title of "Colonel."

When the campaign was over and the ballots cast, the Democrats' hard work and preparations had paid dividends. The Fusionists could not hold together, and were swept from power across the state. A.M. Woodall, editor of the *County Union* in Dunn, was elated.

The newspaper was a mouthpiece of the Democratic Party, and the editorial page of the November 9, 1898 edition was full of gleeful accounts about their success. "Tuesday was a grand day for North Carolina. The white men of the State went to battle with ballots for white supremacy and good government. When the sun had set the victory was won. . . . In Harnett County our chairman, Mr. J.C. Clifford, has the thanks of 1650 white voters for the magnificent and efficient manner in which he led us to victory."

Woodall was not above gloating over his party's success, pointing out, "You can tell a fusionist now by the length of his face. Few of them wear smiles now. Poor fellows, they died hard." The last comment was perhaps the most accurate of all, for the Populists had fought a close fight in all county races despite the racial scare tactics of the Democrats. In most races across the county, the margin of victory was less than 200 votes.

For the next 30 years, there was parity among the political parties in Harnett, as the Populist Party disintegrated and many of its members were compelled to choose between the Democrats or Republicans. Most cast their lots with the Republicans. Republicans held several offices during the first 30 years of the twentieth century, but were unable to totally oust the Democrats again until 1928.

HANNIBAL GODWIN

A Harnett native who rose to prominence during this period was Hannibal Godwin. Born November 3, 1873, the son of Archibald and Rebecca Godwin grew up on his family's farm near Dunn. Godwin graduated from Trinity College (now Duke University), studied law in Chapel Hill, and in 1896 returned to his hometown to set up his law practice. Godwin began his political career in 1897 when he was elected mayor of Dunn. Five years later, he was elected to the North Carolina Senate by the people of the 15th District, which in 1902 included Harnett, Sampson, and Johnston Counties. Godwin served only one term in the State Senate but remained active within the Democratic Party after his term expired, serving on the State Executive Committee from 1904 to 1906. He was nominated to be a presidential elector in 1904.

When the Democrats from the 6th Congressional District held their convention in 1906, Godwin received the nomination to be their candidate for Congress.

He was a "compromise candidate," as the Democratic leadership wanted to avoid a potentially brutal contest unfolding among some of the more powerful politicians who wanted the nomination. Hannibal Godwin easily defeated his Republican opponent in the general election and became the first person from Harnett to serve in the U.S. Congress.

Godwin served seven terms in Congress, ending his career at the ripe old age of 47. His longevity in office is attributable to the close contact he maintained with the people of his district. Often he found himself at odds with his party's leadership, but the people he represented were always pleased with his service. Historian John Oates wrote of Godwin, "He was very popular with the voters. It is said that he sent a picture of his family each two years to the voters of the district and each term there was another child added to the picture. The people wanted that kind of man to represent them."

1900–1910 POPULATION INFORMATION

The census of 1900 found 15,988 people residing in Harnett County. Of the two incorporated towns, Dunn held the largest population with 1,072 inhabitants. The county seat, Lillington, had a permanent population of 65.

When the U.S. Census was taken in 1910, Harnett's population had grown to 22,174. The county now had five incorporated towns, Dunn being the county's largest with 1,823 people. The population of the other towns was Lillington with 380, Buie's Creek with 249, Angier with 221, and Coats was the smallest town with 169.

LILLINGTON BRIDGE

In the first year of the new century, county commissioners continued their efforts to improve the infrastructure of the county. A bond referendum was passed to raise money to construct a bridge across the Cape Fear River at Lillington to replace the old ferry. This was the second attempt to build a structure across the river at the county seat and the third attempt to construct a bridge in what is now Harnett. Officials agreed that once this structure was built, another bridge would be constructed upstream from the Averasboro Ferry.

Commissioners contracted with the Converse Bridge Company of Chattanooga, Tennessee, to build the bridge, and the company promptly dispatched Captain J.W. Hayes to oversee the project. By May 1, 1901, Hayes had located a site that would be firm enough to support the piers and was estimating completion of the project within 60 days.

These unidentified men are standing on the Lillington Bridge during its construction in 1902.

This photograph shows a horse cart crossing the Cape Fear River at Duke c. 1905.

Such predictions were premature. Three weeks later, heavy rains hit the region, sending the Cape Fear on the biggest freshet the river had experienced up to that time; it was dubbed the Prohibition Freshet. One eyewitness noted that during the rain leading up to the flood, the Cape Fear had risen 10 feet in one hour. All of the bridges across streams in western Harnett were carried away, except for one across Lower Little River.

The bridge at Lillington nearly met the same fate as its predecessor, but the water receded before totally carrying away the structure. However, the company did suffer some setbacks. The *Democratic Banner* noted, "We learn that the bridge at Lillington lost about $700 worth of material in the high water last week. About 125 barrels of cement and several thousand feet of lumber were carried down the river."

The freshet led to significant delays in the completion of the bridge. Finally, on December 24, 1901, the last bolts were tightened and Captain J.H. Wilson, who had replaced Hayes, proclaimed the bridge complete and ready for traffic. Register of Deeds A.C. Holloway and Fannie Reid McKay were the first to cross the bridge as a crowd of 200 people looked on.

Oscar J. Spears, who was also present, wrote the following description:

> This bridge is of steel except the approaches; and consists of three spans of equal length, which are each one hundred and sixty-one feet, and from land to land the total length is seven hundred and thirteen feet. From the average water height to the top of the frame work of the bridge is a distance of fifty-six feet. The floor of the bridge standing twenty-nine feet above the average water line four feet above the highest freshet ever known in this age or any time heretofore chronicled by tradition.

The delays led to many cost overruns, and the company erected a tollbooth on the bridge to recoup its losses. The bridge was formally accepted by the county on January 6, 1902. How long the tollbooth remained has not been recorded.

BUIE'S CREEK ACADEMY

In January of 1887, James Archibald Campbell founded a school to educate the children in the Buie's Creek area. The original one-room school was called Buie's Creek Academy and served 21 students from 8 families in the neighborhood. By the year 1900, the academy had grown to the point where it hosted over 100 students. Rooms had been added to the original structure, and a tabernacle built.

A fire on December 21, 1900, destroyed the old Buie's Creek Academy. But thanks to donations and community support, work soon commenced on rebuilding the school. One of the foremost patrons of Reverend Campbell's school was Z.T. Kivett, who had constructed the courthouse in Lillington. Kivett moved his family to the site of the academy, set up a brick kiln, and commenced construction. The brick building that resulted was known as Kivett Hall and was completed in November of 1903. It was reputed to be the largest brick building in the county at the time. The academy continued to grow and prosper. Reverend Dr. Campbell transferred the school to the North Carolina Baptist State Convention in 1926, and Buies Creek Academy became Campbell Junior College. Under the leadership of Dr. Leslie Campbell, the founder's son, the school attained senior college status in 1961.

The settlement around the academy grew until it was finally deemed advantageous to incorporate the village. On March 4, 1903, the Town of Buie's Creek was officially incorporated by the General Assembly. The first town officers named included Mayor John McKay Byrd, and Commissioners Rufus Barbee, J.F. McLeod, W.H. Upchurch, and F.H. Taylor. These men were to serve until the first official election could be held, which was slated for "the first Tuesday in May, one thousand nine hundred and three." All men originally named were elected that May to continue serving in their respective posts.

The law creating the town contained a clause that prohibited the sale of cigarettes or "any paper for the purpose of making cigarettes." Another section banned alcohol, and another stipulated that it would be illegal for doctors to even

This is an early image of the Kivett building at Campbell University.

prescribe alcohol in Buie's Creek "except the same be given for a person *bona fide* sick under his charge."

CAPE FEAR AND NORTHERN RAILROAD

Jonathan Cicero Angier operated extensive sawmill operations in southern Wake County, and his plant in Cary was an important source of lumber in the Raleigh area. In an effort to exploit the timber forests that stretched south into Harnett, Angier constructed a railroad south from Apex in 1899. This short line was called the Cape Fear and Northern Railroad. The southern terminus for the line was on the farm of Jake Williams, who operated a general store and turpentine distillery nearby.

The arrival of the railroad provided a convenient and reliable transportation artery, and it became a popular mode of transportation with the farmers in the area.

In July of 1899, streets and lots were laid off by surveyor Dan Green on Williams's farm in the vicinity of the railroad terminus. Lots were sold at an August 1899 celebration, which a writer for the *News and Observer* described as "a big day." Speeches were given by prominent individuals, and the brass band from Dunn provided music. The new town was called Angier in honor of the man who brought the railroad into the northeastern part of Harnett County. Angier was officially incorporated by the North Carolina General Assembly in 1901. The first mayor was Jake Williams, and M.W. Denning was named chief of police. W.H. Gregory, B.F. Williams, and C.S. Adams were town commissioners.

Angier prospered, especially after 1902 when Jonathan Angier relocated most of his lumber operations to the town. A writer for the *Democratic Banner* observed on September 11, 1901, "Angier is only three years old and during that time wonderful improvements have been made. They have eight or ten stores which do a fairly good business."

In 1902, Angier decided to continue his line south further into the pine forests of northeastern Harnett that had once produced copious amounts of naval stores. He wanted to connect his line with Fayetteville but was unsure which route to choose. Finally, he decided to continue his line to Dunn and there to link up with the Atlantic Coast Line Railroad. To help him make his decision, town leaders in Dunn gave Angier land for a lumber mill.

By the summer of 1903 the line was complete from Durham to Dunn. A large celebration in honor of the event was held in Dunn and was described by a writer for the *Fayetteville Observer*: "Between 5,000 and 6,000 patriotic North Carolinians thronged that progressive town Thursday to join citizens of Dunn in their celebration of the advent of the Cape Fear and Northern Railway. Mr. John C. Angier, who planned and built the road, was the hero of the hour. Excursions were run from Raleigh and Durham, and hundreds went from Fayetteville and other points on the Atlantic Coast Line, while every section of old Harnett was represented."

Troyville was in existence at a site along the Raleigh to Fayetteville Stage Road as early as July of 1877, for that was when a post office was established there with Joseph A. Stewart as postmaster. When surveyors for the Cape Fear and Northern came through the area scouting for a route to extend the line, they dropped by the store of James T. Coats, who owned over 700 acres of land in and around Troyville. Coats was enthusiastic about the prospects of the rail line passing through the community, and not only gave the company right of way across his land, he also gave land for a depot. Land around the depot was laid out soon thereafter into a new town with regular streets, and business and residential lots.

The town was named Coats, in honor of James T. Coats, and was officially incorporated by the legislature on March 4, 1905. The first town officers were J.K. Stewart, mayor; and R.M. Coats, J.G. Stephens, J.W. Talton, and W.H. Coats, commissioners. These men were appointed to serve until the first town elections could be held on the first Monday in May 1905.

A spur line was completed shortly thereafter to Duke, providing a transportation outlet for the fabric being produced at Erwin Mills. In 1906, the Cape Fear and Northern became the Durham and Southern Railway. Portions of Angier's railroad served the people of Harnett County until the dawn of the twenty-first century.

THE FOUNDING OF ERWIN MILLS

The impetus for the most extensive and elaborate industrial scheme ever undertaken in Harnett County actually began in Durham County on April 20, 1892, when the Erwin Cotton Mill Company was chartered. Several members of the prominent Duke family, renowned throughout the world for their tobacco operations, formed the company in an effort to diversify their holdings. Cotton mills were a natural sideline for them, as the cotton sheeting was needed for tobacco.

After erecting their first mill in Durham, the company cast about looking for sites on which to build other mills. A site near Smiley's Falls on the Cape Fear River in Harnett County caught their eye. The Smiley's Falls Manufacturing Company had been trying unsuccessfully for nearly 20 years to harness the power of the Cape Fear in some type of manufacturing operation at the site. After many setbacks, mostly due to financial problems, they were looking to give up their extensive investigations of the falls and its waterpower potential to entice the Erwin Cotton Mill Company to come to the site. The fact that cotton was grown extensively in the surrounding area made the site even more appealing to the Dukes.

In the first few years of the new century, the Erwin Cotton Mill Company acquired several thousand acres of land along the Cape Fear in the vicinity of Smiley's Falls. Finally, in the summer of 1902, word of the company's plans was reported to the public. In the August 6, 1902 *Democratic Banner* the operations were described as follows:

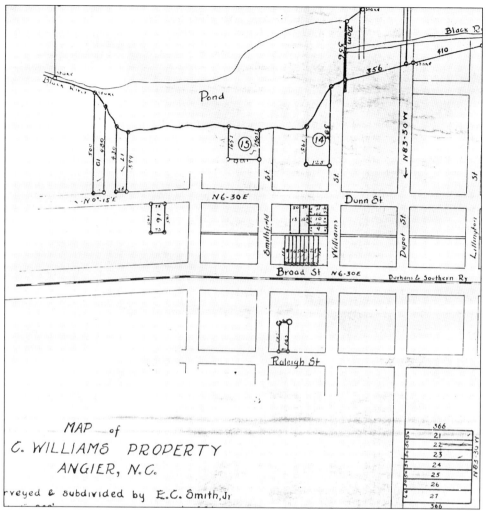

This 1921 map shows downtown Angier.

It has been ascertained that the Erwin Cotton Mills Company will, in a few months, erect near Smiley's Falls on the Cape Fear River about four miles from the city, a mammoth cotton mill. The mill will manufacture denim and will have about 70,000 spindles and 2,000 looms. It will give employment to about 2,000 hands. Engineers have begun to lay off streets and arrange for water supply, electric lights and everything necessary to make an ideal town. The houses will be better than any yet constructed in the State for operations.

On August 16, 1902, the "hub stake" was driven in the middle of the proposed town, near where the E.R. Thomas Drug Company building would one day stand, and work on laying out the site began. Work on Erwin Cotton Mill #2 and

300 houses in the mill town commenced shortly after the streets were laid out. Construction lasted for more than a year. A temporary village of makeshift shacks to house the workers building the mill grew up along Colvin's Branch and was called Erwin, in honor of William A. "Bill" Erwin, the supervisor of construction operations who became manager of the mill after it was opened. But the new town was officially designated Duke, in honor of the Duke family of Durham who played such a prominent role in the company.

The mill went into operation in 1904. According to historian Sion. Harrington III: "Named for Bill Erwin, the mill boasted 1,024 looms and some 35,000 spindles. In 1906, the mill began producing the cloth which ultimately made Erwin 'The Denim Capital of the World.' "

THE COUNTY SEAT GETS A RAILROAD

The Raleigh and Cape Fear Railway was chartered in February of 1898 for the purpose of connecting Raleigh and Fayetteville by rail. The route of the line cut across the middle of Harnett, following much the same path laid out for the proposed but never completed Metropolitan Railroad in 1846.

The founders of Erwin Mills were photographed at Duke in the summer of 1904. Shown from left to right: (front row) B.N. Duke, W. Duke, J.B. Duke, T.J. Walker, J.W. Goodson, unidentified, and Jonathan Angier; (back row) Dr. A.G. Carr, W.A. Erwin, J.E. Stagg, Frank Tate, E.S. Yarborough, George Lemmon, and F.L. Fuller. (Courtesy North Carolina Department of Archives and History.)

This is a 1904 schedule from the Raleigh and Cape Fear Railroad.

RALEIGH & CAPE FEAR R. R.

Schedule Effective April! 5, 1904.

Train 101 (second-class) leaves Raleigh 7:20 a. m;. arrive C. F. & N. Junction 9:20 a. m.; arrives Lillington Station 10:25 a. m.

Train 105 (first-class) leaves Raleigh 4:15 p. m.; arrives C. F. & N. Junction 5:22 p. m.; arrives Lillington 6:10 p. m.

Train 104 (first-class) leaves Lillington 7:45 a. m.; leaves C. F. & N. Junction 8:33 a. m.; arrives Raleigh 9:45 a. m.

Train 102 (second-class) leaves Lillington 3:50 p. m.; leaves C. F. & N. Junction 4:55 p. m.; arrives Raleigh 6:35 p. m.

The new railroad moved south from Wake County, and construction crews reached the Cape Fear River across from Lillington by February of 1903. By July of that year, a bridge was constructed across the river and the railroad arrived in the county seat amidst much celebrations. Shortly after reaching the Cape Fear, a barge service was instituted with points along the river as far upstream as Buckhorn. Merchandise could be transferred from rail to barge at Lillington and shipped to folks along the river. How long this service was offered is unknown.

Eventually, the line was extended south to Fayetteville. The Raleigh and Cape Fear was merged with the Raleigh and Southport in 1905 and, in 1911, was absorbed by the Norfolk Southern Railroad. This became an important transportation artery for the county, and many communities grew along the railroad sidings, including Fonville, Harnett, Bunnlevel, Chalybeate Springs, Kipling, and Rawls.

When the railroad made it as far south as Bradley's Store, citizens of the community held a meeting to decide what to name the railroad station and depot erected just south of the store. N.A. Smith, a prominent resident of the area who had served in the General Assembly, proposed naming it in honor of his favorite author, Rudyard Kipling. Everyone agreed, and Kipling was born.

A few miles to the north, the community of Chalybeate Springs was officially created at roughly the same time, but its creation was more thought out. By the end of the nineteenth century, a mineral spring here was known as Betts Spring, but it was also known at least as early as the War Between the States as Chalybeate Springs. By 1902, the land came into the ownership of J.R. Franklin and D.H. Senter, who hired surveyor Walter Byrd to lay out a town on the 100 acres of land around the springs. Soon this was a bustling community complete with stores, a lumber mill, and a railroad depot. The springs were developed into a tourist attraction, and visitors from Raleigh rode the train to spend time partaking of the healthful benefits of the mineral water. The town takes its unusual name from the iron content found in the water.

An important community in Harnett for many years, "Bunlevel" was officially incorporated by the North Carolina General Assembly on December 14, 1921. The first officers were L.A. Bethune, mayor; and John McD. Parker, J.W. Byrd, and B.F. Truelove, commissioners. On February 23, 1922, a writer for the *Harnett County News* observed, "Bunnlevel has 300 inhabitants and seven stores. It is situated on the Norfolk Southern Railway between Lillington and Linden. It is one of the most progressive of Harnett's settlements and is a very important trading center."

WESTERN HARNETT PROSPERS

In the western portion of the county, the people were also experiencing a wave of prosperity. In 1883, the Western Railroad was absorbed by the Cape Fear and Yadkin Valley Railway, which in 1900 became a part of the Atlantic Coast Line Railroad. The line had been extended north to Greensboro, opening service between that city in the Piedmont and Wilmington on the coast. This led to a significant increase of traffic along the line across western Harnett, and many of the old rail sidings such as Rock Branch, Pineview, and Spout Springs prospered.

Swann Station, "lying partly in the county of Moore and partly in the county of Harnett," was incorporated by the General Assembly on March 7, 1901. The original officers appointed were William Woodall, mayor; J.M. Monroe, A.C. Womack, and N.C. McFadyen, commissioners; and D.H. Morris, constable.

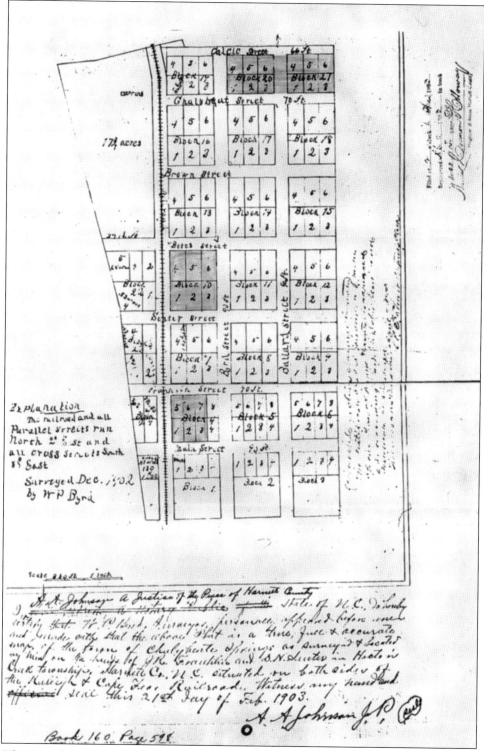

This is Walter Byrd's 1902 plat of Chalybeate Springs.

Apparently this incorporation did not work out, for ten years later on March 4, 1911 the General Assembly incorporated Swann's (the "Station" was dropped). A new set of officers were appointed, including G.F. Myers, mayor; Louis McLeod, George Morris, William Holder, and John Cameron, commissioners; and J.M. Monroe, constable.

In the year 1906, W.W. Giles came into the Sandhills looking to make money, and he purchased 1,200 acres of land from a man named Mayne, a fellow Northerner who had bought the land from Rory Barnes and began raising Angora goats. Giles, however, had loftier goals than becoming a goatherd. He established a health resort known as Eden Colony, subdividing his land into town lots and laying out 60 plots on both sides of the railroad. He also set aside a large plot for people to take their daily exercises on. This was shown on subsequent surveys as the "reservation lawn."

The project revolved around the cultivation of the dewberry, a relative of the blackberry that was one of the most important crops grown in the Sandhills prior to the introduction of tobacco. Dewberries were described in Giles's promotional literature in the following terms: "The dewberry is usually 1 1/2 inches long and 2 inches in diameter. Plants for one acre cost $6.80. Planted in early spring has a crop in 15 months worth from $150 to $750. There are but few crops on earth so profitable and quickly produced."

Giles was an able promoter, sending pamphlets, brochures, and cards throughout the North. One such card says this of his resort: "A newly discovered health resort at Rock Branch, North Carolina, surrounded by Eden Colony, the place where invalids go and get well without medicine; and then make $200 per acre raising fruit. Descriptive booklet of lots and prices free." The reverse side continues the glowing description, "Diseases of the throat, lungs and stomach gradually disappear without medicine at Rock Branch, N.C."

To lure passersby, Giles erected a large sign across from the railroad depot that proclaimed, "Rock Branch is the place where the invalids come and get well without medicine. Good land on easy terms." Leon MacDonald, a historian of the region, recalled the story of a fellow from Ohio named Willard Bicker who had come south seeking the wonders of Eden Colony. He later became disenchanted with the place, and one day drew a large "H" on a piece of paper, then walked over and pasted it over the "W" in Giles's sign. "That's more like it," he proclaimed.

The advertising efforts of Giles paid off for Eden Colony in the short run, as several Northerners in addition to Bicker came to the resort. However, the demand for dewberries died off prior to World War I, and the resort lost one of its main drawing cards.

TRANSPORTATION IMPROVES

In May of 1911, Upper Little River, Neill's Creek, and Lillington Townships overwhelmingly approved a bond referendum to raise $65,000 for the construction of a railroad connecting Lillington and Sanford. The line was called

This is a photograph of Eden Colony c. 1910. (Courtesy North Carolina Department of Archives and History.)

the Atlantic and Western Railroad, commonly known as the A&W, and was operated by John A. Mills and W.J. Edwards. When news of the new rail line to Lillington spread, a writer for the *News & Observer* noted, "Ten years ago it was easier to go to New York from Raleigh than to go to Lillington, and Harnett county was without railroad facilities except on two borders."

The Atlantic and Western began service in 1903 from Sanford to Jonesboro, in Lee County. A year later, the line was extended east to Broadway. With the approval of the bond referendum in Harnett, it was decided to push the line into Lillington. Ultimately, the company hoped to extend their tracks as far east as Goldsboro.

By April of 1913, the line stretched 26.5 miles between Lillington and Sanford. Small communities grew up at stops along the route, and the rail owners hoped that these would develop into thriving towns. Rail sidings in Harnett included Seminole, Ryes, Arlington, Mamers, and Luart. Of these, Mamers was the most substantial.

The A&W began service between Sanford and Lillington with two locomotives in 1913. By the 1940s they were using three steam locomotives and two "jitneys," or single-car passenger carriers. The company stayed in business for half a century, but like many of the short line railroads, the A&W was unable to compete with the trucking industry. The line was discontinued, and on December 15, 1961, the A&W made its final run from Lillington to Sanford.

RAILROAD ACROSS NORTHERN HARNETT

The Raleigh, Charlotte and Southern Railway was chartered in the spring of 1911 for the purpose of creating a rail line connecting Raleigh and Charlotte. To accomplish this, the company acquired several small, local railroads, then built lines to fill in the blank spots. One such gap existed between Varina and Colon. This 23-mile section, which cut across the northern portion of Harnett, was completed by the end of 1912. The company erected a depot in the county and called it Duncan, which became an important transportation hub for people living in northern Harnett.

The Norfolk Southern Railroad absorbed the Raleigh, Charlotte and Southern Railway on January 1, 1914. In 1917, the Durham and South Carolina Railroad, which operated a short track stretching from Durham across eastern Chatham

This 1910 postcard shows a fruit grower's cottage in Eden Colony. (Courtesy North Carolina Department of Archives and History.)

County, constructed an extension into Harnett. This joined their railroad to the Norfolk Southern at Duncan and provided a valuable rail outlet for tobacco markets in Durham. This line remained an important artery across the central part of the state into the 1970s.

BOUNDARY SHIFT OF 1911

As law enforcement became more efficient in the Dunn area during the early years of its existence, many of the troublesome grog shops and taverns moved out of town to an area just across the Cumberland County line and set up operations. Here they were relatively safe. They were beyond the jurisdiction of the Harnett sheriff, and the Cumberland sheriff had little incentive to get involved in the goings on in the northeastern fringe of his county as he had his hands full maintaining order in Fayetteville.

To bring order to this rowdy area, the General Assembly passed a law in 1911 annexing the northeastern corner of Cumberland to Harnett. To accomplish this they decreed that the county line should no longer run from the mouth of Lower Little River to the spot where the Johnston/Sampson line intersected Mingo Swamp.

Instead, the new county line was delineated as follows: "Thence with the line of Sampson County, that is to say down the various courses of Black Mingo to Lightwood Knot bridge over said Black Mingo; thence a direct line to the mouth of Lower Little River."

JARVIS COUNTY

For many who resided in Dunn, the boundary shift was purely academic, for they were intent on becoming a county seat. Their efforts to remove the courthouse from Lillington had met with failure for more than 25 years. If they could not become the county seat of Harnett, they reasoned, then they would become the seat of a new county.

A movement began in 1912 to create North Carolina's 101st county. The citizens began their efforts with the customary petitions and speeches. Their work culminated with a measure introduced into the North Carolina General Assembly in 1917 by Representative George Grantham of Harnett. The new county was to be called Jarvis, in honor of former Governor William Jarvis, who served as governor from 1879 to 1885.

It is ironic that the new county was named for a Democratic governor, as most of those who opposed creating the new county did so on the grounds that it would create a new Republican stronghold. Had the county been created, it would have taken Harnett east of Neill's Creek and the Cape Fear River. In addition, it would have included the northeastern portion of Cumberland, the northwestern portion of Sampson and the southwestern portion of Johnston. Dunn, of course, would have been the county seat.

This c. 1900 photograph shows East Broad Street in Dunn.

John C. Clifford, a former representative from Harnett and aide to Congressman Hannibal Godwin, was the bill's most ardent supporter. John A. Oates of Fayetteville, a former mayor of Dunn, was its most vocal antagonist. Clifford and Oates had been friends for many years, having been classmates during college at Wake Forest. In the end, Oates and his followers were successful. House Bill H1083 passed through both houses of the legislature but was killed in a committee before it could be ratified.

Undaunted, the citizens of Dunn continued their efforts to make their town a county seat into the 1920s, but they were never as close as they had been in 1917. The final effort came in 1921, when the town proposed that a referendum be held in Harnett to remove the county seat from Lillington. The town even offered to sell to the county for $1 the courthouse building they had constructed in anticipation of being the Jarvis County seat. But the effort failed.

SOIL SURVEY OF 1917

As a joint project of the North Carolina Department of Agriculture and the U.S. Department of Agriculture, Robert Jurney and S.O. Perkins conducted a study of the soils in Harnett throughout 1916. The duo published the results of their work in 1917 under the title, *Soil Survey of Harnett County, North Carolina.*

Their report begins with a description of Harnett's geography, listing the various physiographic regions, creeks, streams, and swamps. It even mentions the two largest towns and gives their respective populations—Dunn with 1,823 and Duke with 500. The geographic report did contain one major error though. The elevation of Lillington was given as 635 feet above sea level, when in actuality it only averages about 225 feet. This miscalculation gave rise to the myth that Lillington is the highest county seat in the eastern part of the state.

The most important part of the survey, at least from a historical point of view, was the part dealing with Harnett agriculture. There were 2,710 farms in the county, the average farm in those days being 90.8 acres. Some lumber holdings in the Sandhills, though, did reach as high as 54,000 acres. The description of the farm implements with which Harnett farmers worked their lands back then was also interesting.

> The farm equipment, as a rule, consists mainly of 1-horse implements, including turning plows, cultivators, spike-tooth harrows, cotton and corn planters, fertilizer distributors and stalk cutters. Some of the better farms have improved labor-saving machinery, such as disk plows, disk harrows, weeders, manure spreaders, reapers, riding cultivators and land

Hog killings were important events on Harnett farms well into the twentieth century.

rollers. Both horses and mules are used for work stock, mules predominating. The farm buildings are for the most part small, but some of the better improved farms have large, well-equipped barns.

Cotton and corn were the leading crops in Harnett in 1916. Over 20,000 acres were planted with cotton and 31,000 with corn. By contrast, tobacco was only grown on 219 acres in the county. "Cotton and corn are still the most extensively grown crops in the county, cotton being the most important cash crop," the survey said. "Tobacco is also a cash crop, but it is of little importance on account of small acreage." There was also some interesting information about Harnett's fruits and nuts. "In 1910 there were 23,354 apple trees, 19,542 peach trees, 2,934 grapevines, and 17 acres of blackberries and dewberries in the county. The total value of fruits and nuts produced in 1909 was $40,208."

To accompany their report, Jurney and Perkins produced a large, full-color map showing the location of various soil types as well as other features around Harnett. The map is significant in that it is the earliest drawn specifically of Harnett.

This Farmer's Union meeting was held at Erwin's Chapel Church in 1905. (Courtesy North Carolina Department of Archives and History.)

GRANVILLE WILT

During this era, many individuals began moving into Harnett from the northern section of North Carolina. They were tobacco farmers looking for a place to start new farms, and the soils of Harnett beckoned. These farmers had been driven from their native region by a bacterial disease known as Granville Wilt, so named because it was first identified on the farm of B.F. Stem in Granville County in 1881.

Scientists spent nearly 60 years trying to overcome the pestilence. The farmers who settled in Harnett County found the land mostly safe from the disease.

The most notable of these tobacco farmers who migrated into Harnett was Will Olive. A Chatham County native, Olive had become adept at growing tobacco while living in Rockingham County. When his job with the Cape Fear and Yadkin Valley Railroad brought him to Sanford in 1911, he soon found in the Sandhills of Lee and Harnett an area suitable for the production of bright leaf tobacco.

In 1912, Olive purchased 600 acres of land at Rock Branch for $5,000 and immediately set about developing the land for the cultivation of tobacco. He subdivided the parcel and sold tracts to other farmers who wanted to try their luck growing tobacco.

The community prospered, and thanks to Olive's tireless promotional efforts, other industries moved into the area, including the Never Fail Can Company (a manufacturer of oil cans) and the H.C. Cameron Lumber Company. In honor of Will Olive's efforts, folks around Rock Branch changed the name of their community to Olivia.

WORLD WAR I

On June 28, 1914, 19-year-old Guarilo Princip assassinated the Archduke Franz Ferdinand and his wife the Duchess of Hohenburg in Sarajevo. This episode was the catalyst of the war now known as World War I. Within two months of Princip's deed, eight nations from throughout Europe were embroiled in a war that would eventually cost nearly 17 million soldiers and an estimated 12.5 million civilians their lives.

Nearly three years later, President Woodrow Wilson and the U.S. Congress officially entered the United States in the fray on the side of Great Britain and France. By the time the war was over on November 11, 1918, the decision would cost the United States more than 300,000 casualties.

As usual, North Carolina responded vigorously to the call to arms. The Old North State contributed 86,457 troops to the war effort, of which 5,799 became casualties and 1,610 were killed outright. Harnett County lost its share of men among the trenches of Europe. It is known that at least 766 of her sons went to war.

Thirty-seven never returned, giving their lives in what many called "The War to End All Wars."

This is a portrait of Mayton Upchurch in his World War I–era uniform. He was the last surviving veteran of the war in Harnett County. (Courtesy Sion Harrington III.)

Historian Sion Harrington III, who has conducted extensive research on Harnett's role in World War I, noted three individuals whose accomplishments stood out during the war:

> Sergeant Julius Johnson of Duke was awarded the British Military Medal for bravery. This is the third highest medal awarded by the British Army to enlisted men.
>
> Corporal Charles Stevenson of Angier was awarded the Distinguished Service Cross for single-handedly attacking several Germans. This medal is second only to the Congressional Medal of Honor.
>
> Ollie Link of Buie's Creek got one of each. He was a cook in Co. M, 119th Infantry, and during the battle of St. Souplet in France he left the kitchen to help carry wounded men from the battlefield while under enemy fire. Later in the battle he advanced 200 yards into enemy territory to locate German machine gun positions. For this, Link was awarded both the British Military Medal and the Distinguished Service Cross.

The first man from Harnett killed in battle during this war was William H. Matthews, who lived near Kipling. He was killed near the Marne River on July 18, 1918. This fact was unknown to those who organized an elaborate ceremony at Prospect Church on October 31, 1920, when Private Jesse Avery's remains were buried after having been returned from Belgium, where he had been killed on August 5, 1918. Most county officials thought Avery was the first of Harnett's sons to lose his life in the war, hence the large patriotic ceremony.

8. ROARING TWENTIES AND THE GREAT DEPRESSION

The population of Harnett County continued a slow but steady rise in the period between 1920 and 1940. Census figures show that in 1920 the population was 28,313; in 1930 it was 37,911; and in 1940 it had grown to 44,239. Although still very much a rural county, Harnett was starting to see changes that would have profound effects on the way people lived their lives. Chief among these changes was improved transportation, both on the ground and in the air.

GROWTH OF FORT BRAGG

In the spring of 1918, Major General William J. Snow, chief of artillery for the U.S. Army, dispatched Colonel E.P. King on a mission through the Southeast looking for an appropriate place to establish an artillery training post. Colonel King was impressed with the Sandhills region of North Carolina, despite the fact that the region was a veritable wilderness. "At that time there were no maps such as we have today and we found very few sign posts through the country," King later recalled. "The Geological Survey had made very few maps in that section. We traveled principally by compass and dead reckoning." Colonel King made his way to Manchester and then Fayetteville, which he used as a base to explore the Sandhills north and west of the city. When he was finished, he had staked out the site for his artillery post. "The area selected begins at a point about ten miles northwest of Fayetteville and extends westward for about twenty-four miles to the vicinity of Southern Pines. Averaging eight miles in width, the reservation contains approximately one hundred twenty-two thousand acres. The post proper was located at the eastern end due to the proximity of the water supply, and the existence of level terrain suitable for drill, maneuvers, post construction, and for airplane landing fields."

The War Department approved the recommendations submitted by Colonel King on July 1, 1918, and Camp Bragg was born. Construction began on September 16, 1918. With the end of World War I it looked, for a time, as though the fledgling camp would soon be closed. But on September 30, 1922, the War

Department made the post permanent, and renamed it Fort Bragg. Today, Fort Bragg has become one of the largest military installations in the world and includes thousands of acres of land, some of which is located in Harnett County. Many residents of the western portion were drawn into the area through their connections to the military at either Fort Bragg or Pope Air Force Base.

OVERHILLS

What was touted as the largest land transfer ever recorded in Harnett County occurred in December of 1921 when the Overhills Land Company acquired 37,000 acres from the Kent-Jordan Company. The land was part of a hunting and recreational resort located in the southwestern part of the county that became a favored retreat for members of the Rockefeller family.

The Overhills estate had once been a portion of a turpentine plantation owned by the McDiarmid family and was traversed by both the Fayetteville and Western Plank Road and the Western Railroad. In 1901, the land was purchased from Consolidated Lumber Company by William Johnston, who hoped to turn the land into a hunting preserve called "Arranmore." Johnston's plans fell through, and in 1906, his son sold the 22,000 acres to the Croatan Club.

The Croatan Club, a corporation of businessmen and friends of the founders General John Gill and James Woodard, had grand plans for developing the tract

This c. 1925 image of Overhills Country Club shows Harriman Cottage in middle and Covert Cottage on right. (Courtesy North Carolina Department of Archives and History.)

This photograph of Percy Rockefeller at Overhills was taken c. 1925. (Courtesy North Carolina Department of Archives and History.)

into a world-class resort community. An article in the November 15, 1906 *Fayetteville Observer* described the property and their plans:

> The tract is in the vicinity of Manchester, in this county, and is partly divided by the Atlantic & Yadkin division of the A.C.L. which runs through it. There are 8,000 acres of arable land in the purchase. These will be cultivated in corn, wheat, buckwheat, hay and other necessities for the wild game, but none of the product will be harvested for market. There is a lake of 500 acres on the property. The new clubhouse will overlook this and will contain all the comforts of an up-to-date residence. It will be arranged to accommodate the families of the members and their friends.

The club never developed to their expectations, and by 1910 the group sold the property to James Jordan and Leonard Tufts for $75,000. Tufts sold his interest to California Congressman William Kent, who formed the Kent-Jordan Company with his fellow owner in 1911. By acquiring adjacent farms and landholdings, they amassed more than 35,000 acres of land, which was transferred to the Overhills Land Company in 1921.

119

In 1913, the Kent-Jordan Company established the Overhills Country Club. They built roads and trails on the tract and stocked ponds for fishing. They also erected stables and kennels needed to house the animals used in fox hunting. A town called "Pinewild" was envisioned for the site but never came into being. The focal point of their development was a large clubhouse, which overlooked a golf course created by the famous course designer Donald Ross and which was completed by the spring of 1916.

Many wealthy guests came to visit the Overhills Country Club, the most significant being Percy Rockefeller, who made his first visit there in 1916. Another visitor was William Averill Harriman, a renowned polo player who later became governor of New York. It was his influence that led to the resort becoming one of the premier polo facilities in the South during the 1920s. Rockefeller and Harriman were the founders of the Overhills Land Company, and were the owners of the estate during its most active period.

Overhills was world renowned during the 1920s as one of the premiere locales for fox-hunting. Hunters and hounds would gather at the circular area known as the Great Circus before riding out in pursuit of the fox.

The Great Depression brought an end to the large-scale sporting events at Overhills. The estate eventually became a private retreat for the Rockefeller family, who maintained ownership of the property until it was sold to the U.S. Army in 1997.

HIGHWAY EXPANSION

In 1924, John A. Oates of Fayetteville, a former mayor of Dunn, convinced three influential gentlemen from Fayetteville—A.E. Dixon, B.R. Huske, and Major H.O. Pond—of the benefits of a direct motor highway linking Jacksonville, Florida, with Richmond, Virginia, following the route of the Atlantic Coast Line Railroad. These men traveled to towns and cities all along the proposed route, giving speeches and presentations advocating the new highway. Ultimately, they were successful in their quest.

The route chartered was designated N.C. Route 22 from Rowland to Wilson. In 1927, when the federal government created a series of routes through the respective states known as U.S. highways, N.C. 22 became a part of U.S. Route 217. In 1932, U.S. 217 from Wilson to South Carolina and U.S. Route 17-1 from Wilson to Virginia were merged and given the designation of U.S. Route 301, which for many years served as one of the main transportation arteries along the eastern seaboard, linking the cities of the northeast with Tampa Bay, Florida.

Another important highway cutting across Harnett County was constructed during this period. Route 60, later known as U.S. Route 421, crossed North Carolina from northwest to southeast, connecting cities and towns such as Boone, Winston-Salem, Greensboro, Sanford, Clinton, and Wilmington. As it traversed Harnett, Route 60 passed through Dunn, Erwin, Buie's Creek, Lillington, Mamers, and Seminole.

In September of 1925, Henderson Steele of the *Harnett County News* described the technique used by the crews as they surfaced the road through Lillington. "The cause of the great dust clouds was the sweeping of the street preparatory to laying on oil and tar paving. A giant sweeper is first run over the roadway in order to thoroughly clean the surface when it covers the face of the road. Then the 'tar wagon', a large motor tank car, comes along and sprays the heated mixture. Next come the shovelmen who throw sand upon the tar, and the absorption and hardening process begins."

Shortly after its completion, Route 60 was designated as the "Boone Trail Highway" in honor of the fact that Daniel Boone had lived in the vicinity of the road in its northwestern section. In several towns along the route, large arrowhead-shaped memorials built with rocks were erected to commemorate Boone. The memorials were the idea of Hampton Rich, who designed and built the markers. Rich built at least three of these markers in Harnett County—in Dunn, Lillington, and Erwin. There are some claims that a fourth monument stood in the Boone Trail community, but so far no evidence or pictures of the marker have been located.

Another north/south thoroughfare that passed through Harnett County was constructed during the mid-1920s. Called the Lafayette Highway in honor of

These foresters held their 1924 annual meeting at Overhills. (Courtesy North Carolina Department of Archives and History.)

Revolutionary War hero the Marquis de Lafayette, it connected Raleigh and Fayetteville by passing through Chalybeate Springs, Lillington, Kipling, and Bunnlevel. Today, this road is known as U.S. Route 401.

On September 1, 1925, W.D. Somervill inspected a new highway that had been constructed across western Harnett connecting Jonesboro with Fort Bragg. He described the road as "natural sand clay and is a very good job with good smooth riding surface." The only delay in the project was the painting of guardrails, which Somervill noted was being "held up on account of weather being so dry that it is impossible to get a decent paint job on account of the dust. This painting will be completed after the first rain." This road, now known as N.C. Route 87, became an important thoroughfare connecting Sanford with Fayetteville. As the twenty-first century dawns, work crews are busily converting the two-lane road into a four-lane highway.

Early Aviation

The first encounters with flying machines in Harnett County came during World War I and the years immediately following the war. Military aircraft often passed over Harnett on their way to Camp Bragg. Sometimes these planes did not make it and crashed in the county. One such incident was described in the January 9, 1919 edition of the *Harnett County News*:

> Citizens who saw the airplane flying over Lillington late Tuesday afternoon were amazed at the nearness of the machine to the earth, barely skipping treetops, it seemed. As the pilot was crossing Harnett County he was nearing his death, together with two other occupants of the machine. He was probably having trouble and was flying low looking for a place to land.
>
> As the airplane was crossing the Cape Fear River it dropped into the water, exploded, and all lives aboard were lost. There were said to be three men in the machine, but this is probably not known definitely yet, as the bodies have not been recovered as this paper goes to press.

That same year, 1919, another of these military planes was forced to make an emergency landing in a field near Coats. The pilot tried for some time to repair his airplane so he could continue on his way but to no avail. Finally, one of the locals who had gathered to watch the strange spectacle stepped forward and offered his assistance. The young man was Alton Stewart, who until then had never seen an airplane except in a book but who was a proficient automobile mechanic. The pilot was glad to let the young man help.

Upon inspecting the machine, Stewart declared that he would have to break down the motor and rebuild it, a process that would take a week to complete. The motor was repaired and put back in place as scheduled. When the engine was tested and found to be running smoothly, the pilot decided to take the young mechanic up for a ride. From this maiden flight, Stewart developed a passion for aviation. He would go on to become one of the most widely known pilots in the state of North Carolina.

Stewart obtained a surplus military aircraft from the U.S. government. His friend and fellow Coats resident Dr. Harry Roberts also became interested in flying and purchased one of these surplus government planes. The two men became proficient at flying, thanks in part to impromptu lessons from some of the pilots down at Pope Field. Dr. Roberts's enthusiasm was such that he even constructed an airfield and hangar near his home. Tragically, he was killed near Coats when his airplane crashed in 1925.

In 1926, Stewart became the chief pilot at the Marshburn-Robbins Airport, which opened that year south of Raleigh. There he gave flying lessons, participated in air shows, and gave flights to paying passengers. Several notable individuals are known to have flown with Stewart, including Governor Angus McLean, entertainer Will Rogers, and author Ben Dixon MacNeill.

The licensing of civilian pilots was a rare thing in those early days of aviation, and Alton Stewart was one of the earliest pilots to obtain a license to fly in the United States. On April 6, 1926, in a ceremony at the Marshburn-Robbins

This view of Main Street in Angier was photographed in 1923.

Airport, Stewart was given license number 221 issued by the Federal Aeronautique Internationale and certificate number 6,387 by the National Aeronautic Association. Aviation pioneer Orville Wright signed both of these documents. Ben Dixon MacNeill later wrote about the significance of this event, which secured Stewart's place as one of the true trailblazers of aviation in North Carolina: "Not only was Alton Stewart the first aviator to become licensed in North Carolina, he was the 221st licensed pilot in the United States."

The state's best-known civilian pilot was widely regarded for his skill with an aircraft, but fate decreed that his career be a brief one. Tragically, Stewart was killed in a plane crash near Dunn on Christmas Day in 1929. His remains were buried in Coats in a ceremony that drew hundreds of friends from across the state and made the front page of the December 27, 1929 edition of the *News & Observer*. His tombstone sums up the accomplishments of the notable Harnettian: "He died in man's conquest of the air."

COURTHOUSE EXPANSION

Less than 30 years after the new courthouse was completed, county leaders decided it was time to expand the facility. Twenty-one feet were added to the north end of the building. The addition was built in the same fashion as the older part of the building, blending in with the mission-style architecture. The *Harnett County News* described the work in progress in February of 1925 as follows:

> On the first floor in the addition there will be created sufficient room for three more offices and a toilet. Coincident with the building of the addition will be the installation of a modern steam heating system which will be equipped with radiators in each office and the lobby. The boiler will be placed under the jail house.

NEW SCHOOL CONSTRUCTION

As the 1920s began, many small schools were scattered across the county to provide education to the local children. During this decade, an effort to consolidate the small schools into more efficient and modern school facilities was undertaken.

By 1933, there were school districts in the county with modern high school facilities. These community schools were Anderson Creek, Angier, Benhaven, Boone Trail, Buie's Creek, Coats, Dunn, Erwin, Lafayette ,and Lillington. The high schools resulting from the consolidation efforts of this era were to serve the county until the next consolidation push in the 1970s.

Schools for African-American children prior to the era of desegregation were available at Shawtown in Lillington, at Harnett County Training School (Harnett High School) in Dunn, and later at Johnsonville School in western Harnett and Gentry School in Erwin.

These workers were clearing ground to construct a new mill in Duke in 1925.

DUKE GETS A NEW MILL AND A NEW NAME

Construction of a second mill at Duke was completed and ready for operation by January 1, 1925. The 18-month project more than doubled the mill's capacity to produce denim by adding 35,000 spindles. J.L. Crouse and Co. built the structure, with engineers from J.E. Sirrine Co. overseeing the work.

With an estimated population of 2,000, the mill expansion meant more workers would be moving into town and would need a place to stay. Mill officials built more than 300 houses in 1924 to accommodate the new workers and their families. Duke resident and writer Wade Lucas noted in 1925, "Every house in town, together with all the older ones, is being equipped with water and sewerage and each has electric lights. The houses were built primarily for comfort, but no finer houses are in any industrial town."

Another significant change came to Duke at about the same time as the new mill. Beginning on January 1, 1926, the mill town's name was officially changed to Erwin. The Duke family had bestowed a large amount of money on Trinity College, which moved to Durham and became Duke University. The U.S. Postal Service was not happy about having two places in the same state sharing the same name, so the mill town in Harnett County had to find a new name.

CAMERON HILL FIRE TOWER

A group of landowners from southeastern North Carolina came together in the Prince Charles Hotel in Fayetteville in August of 1925 to help protect their valuable forest resources. Known initially as the Timber Owners Forest Protection Association, the group included, "Hugh MacRae interests, the Camp Manufacturing Company, the Overhills Land Co., the Butters Lumber Co., the Beaufort Lumber Co., the D.L. Gore Estate, the Council Tools Co., and a considerable number of smaller owners."

The group chose C.A. Cardwell to serve as chairman, and Hugh McCormick as secretary. It was decided to keep the organization on a temporary basis until 100,000 acres were listed with their group, at which time the Timber Owners Forest Protection Association would be established on a permanent foundation.

Members paid a penny per acre to list their forest land with the organization. Money thus raised was to be matched by funding from "the State and County funds," to help promote the objectives of the group.

Enough money was collected at this initial meeting to pay for the construction of a fire tower atop Cameron's Hill. District Forester K.E. Kimball wrote:

> As a direct result of the cooperation on the part of land owners on a cent an acre, the first fire lookout tower in North Carolina built primarily for that purpose, is about to be erected on Cameron Hill in Harnett County near Pineview. This tower, with the forty or more miles of telephone line which will tie it into the Forest Warden organization, will greatly increase the protection given to the forest lands of Western Harnett County. The tower will overlook a large part of the Fort Bragg Reservation besides parts of Lee, Hoke and Cumberland Counties.

The Cameron Hill Fire Tower was completed in 1926 and has the distinction of being the first fire tower erected by the state of North Carolina on private land. A.F. Graham was the first permanent observer stationed in the outpost, which quickly became a tourist attraction in the region. The first visitors to sign the register were Mrs. D. Sloan, Percy Rockefeller, and Frank Miller. In 1951, the wooden tower was replaced by a 120-foot-tall steel tower built on the south side of N.C. Route 24.

This photograph of the Cameron Hill Fire Tower was taken in 1926. (Courtesy North Carolina Department of Archives and History.)

Paul Green Wins Pulitzer

The Pulitzer Prize for drama was awarded to Harnett native Paul Green in 1927 for his work *In Abraham's Bosom*. The play, subtitled "The Biography of a Negro in Seven Scenes," had been performed at the Provincetown Playhouse and the Garrick Theater in New York in the winter of 1926–1927. The award was of particular significance in this instance, as it was the first time a Pulitzer had been awarded to a Southerner who still resided in the South.

Paul Green was born and raised in Harnett County near Buie's Creek. In his early years, he gained notoriety in the area as an outstanding, ambidextrous baseball pitcher. Following graduation from Buie's Creek Academy in 1914, Green attended the University of North Carolina before being called away to serve in the 30th Division during World War I. Upon his return from service, Green did graduate work in philosophy at both the University of North Carolina (UNC) and Cornell, before returning to UNC as an assistant professor of philosophy. At UNC, Green studied under Professor Frederick Koch and became active in an organization known as the Carolina Playmakers.

Green is perhaps best remembered for his work *The Lost Colony*, a "symphonic drama" he released in 1937 that was performed in an outdoor theater in Manteo. It has been performed every year since World War II. This was the first of several outdoor historical dramas that Green produced.

In addition to receiving the Pulitzer Prize, Green also received several other awards and honors for his literary accomplishments. These include a Gugenheim Fellowship, the Frank P. Graham Award, the North Carolina Award, and the Sir Walter Raleigh Cup. He was named dramatist laureate by the North Carolina General Assembly in 1979.

Lillington Bridge Collapses

By 1930, many people had come to believe the bridge spanning the Cape Fear at Lillington was unsafe. An account from the *Harnett County News* compared the swaying of the bridge resulting from a car crossing it to the "waving motion of a rowboat on the sea." Yet District Highway Commissioner John Hill declared in November 1930 that the structure was safe for travel and fit for a decade's more service.

But Commissioner Hill's optimism was unfounded. On the night of December 13, 1930, the Lillington Bridge collapsed, carrying two cars into the icy waters of the Cape Fear River. Prominent Lillington attorney Neill Ross was driving one of the automobiles.

Considering the fact that the bridge was a conglomeration of earlier structures that had been scrabbled together, there is little wonder that it fell in. A portion of the structure was part of the original bridge built there in 1901. The Freshet of 1908 washed away a large portion of this bridge, as well as Harnett's other bridge at Duke.

This is a portrait of Pulitzer-Prize winner and Harnett native Paul Green.

The surviving section of the 1901 bridge was utilized in the bridge completed in 1909. Mrs. Francis Ross presided over the ribbon cutting ceremony when the Lillington Bridge was dedicated in 1909. Ironically, it was her son Neill Ross who plunged into the Cape Fear when this same bridge collapsed 21 years later.

GREAT DEPRESSION

President Franklin Roosevelt's New Deal Program, whereby economic stimulus was injected into the economy on a large scale, met with a mixed reception across the country. This was true in both North Carolina and Harnett County. Many feared the unprecedented expansion of the federal government and worried that the country was taking a gigantic step toward socialism. Others were glad to see the money and jobs, regardless of future political ramifications.

The New Deal had an unexpected advocate in Harnett County. D.H. Senter had been a Populist or Republican stalwart since the 1890s, serving as chairman of the Board of County Commissioners in 1914. The Chalybeate Springs native was also president of the Bank of Lillington and had been appointed by the county commissioners in 1928 to serve as county manager.

He became disenchanted with the Republican leadership in the county, and he eventually left the party. In 1932, he became a staunch advocate of Roosevelt's New Deal, and by 1940 he had gained enough popularity among his old rivals to secure the nomination for the North Carolina House over incumbent Neill Ross. He went on to beat his former Republican friends in the 1940 general election. For the Republicans, the loss of Senter and the Populist wing of the party was a severe blow. Coupled with the loss of many small farmers who were compelled to change their party affiliation in order to obtain tobacco allotments from Democrat-appointed officials, it would take the Harnett Republicans more than 60 years to recover.

There were several New Deal programs active in Harnett. Organizations such as the National Youth Administration, Works Progress Administration (WPA), and Public Works Administration all were present. The famed Civilian Conservation Corps (CCC) operated throughout the region from a camp set up on the outskirts of Lillington.

Residents in the rural portions of the county received access to electricity during this era thanks to the Rural Electrification Administration, which began putting power lines into the county in the fall of 1941, eventually installing more than 100 miles of cable.

"More than 400 families in Harnett have already filed applications and paid $5 fee for securing electricity for their homes and farms," the *Dunn Dispatch* reported. "The REA lines will cross the Cape Fear River and come into Harnett from Cumberland in the southeastern section of the county. It extends to Bunnlevel, covers the section of Anderson Creek, Stewart's Creek and Upper Little River township which do not have power lines. The REA goes all the way into the Cool Springs and Raven Rock sections."

The town of Dunn profited greatly from several federal programs during the Great Depression. In June of 1936, thanks to the work of Congressman J. Bayard Clark, Dunn received a Congressional appropriation for the construction of a "Federal Building." The town received $86,000, which was used to construct the building on Broad Street that held the U.S. Post Office from 1938 to 1981.

In 1938, Harnett County Commissioners received a grant for $54,000 from the Public Works Administration to be used for the construction of a hospital. The Dunn Hospital was completed in August of 1939 but went unused for more than a year due to a financial oversight—the commissioners had forgotten to ask for an appropriation to cover operational expenses and could not take the money from county funds.

The Dunn Hospital opened on October 1, 1940. In 1956, the name was changed to Betsy Johnson Hospital, Inc., in honor of the mother of hospital benefactor Nathan M. Johnson Sr. This hospital was replaced by a new Betsy Johnson Memorial Hospital that was built on the outskirts of town and officially dedicated in October of 1968.

These rescue crews were on the scene the day the Lillington bridge collapsed.

Russell Hatcher was employed to drag the road near Campbell College in 1930.

In March of 1940, leaders from the North Carolina National Guard inspected the armory in Dunn and found it woefully inadequate. If the facility was not improved, they warned, then the unit could be removed from Dunn.

With this threat looming, Captain James Best set about working to secure funds for a new armory. Best's efforts were successful, as the WPA appropriated $125,000 to build a new armory for the National Guard unit in Dunn. The WPA began work in January of 1941, and the impressive brick structure was finished by Christmas of 1941.

A writer for the *Dunn Dispatch* noted, "The combination armory-community building will give Dunn adequate indoor assembly space for the first time. The auditorium, 75 by 100 feet, will have a seating capacity of 2,000."

WORLD WAR II

On the morning of December 7, 1941, Japanese bombs rained from the sky on the island paradise of Hawaii. This surprise attack was a complete success for the Japanese, and the American military facilities at Pearl Harbor were a total wreck. The United States was plunged into World War II.

Among the 2,403 dead Americans at Pearl Harbor was 25-year-old Sergeant Stanley McLeod, the first person from Harnett County to lose his life in World War II.

As the bombs began to fall upon Hickham Field, McLeod obtained a Thompson submachine gun and headed out onto the parade ground where he began blazing away at Japanese airplanes. During the second wave of their attack, the Japanese concentrated much of their efforts on wiping out the hangars and fuel depot at Hickham Field. As the planes roared in, Sergeant McLeod held his ground, firing the machine gun until he was laid low by a piece of shrapnel from an exploding bomb.

The summer following his death, Sergeant McLeod was posthumously awarded the Distinguished Service Cross for his brave deeds. The medal was presented to his father in a ceremony in front of a crowd of 200 people gathered at the Community Center in Jonesboro.

General John T. Kennedy, commander of Fort Bragg, gave the medal to the elder McLeod and remarked, "I congratulate you personally on raising a boy who was willing to lay down his life without flinching. The heroism of Sgt. Stanley McLeod, acting in defense of his country, is symbolic of the spirit that will enable America to win the war."

Sergeant McLeod was followed by nearly a hundred of his fellow Harnett Countians who gave up their lives for their country during World War II. According to historian Sion Harrington III:

> Unfortunately, figures relating to losses from the county during World War II vary. According to official United States Government figures released in 1946, 63 service members from Harnett County died while serving in the United States Army and Army Air Corps. Eighteen of our own died while serving in the United States Navy, Coast Guard, and Marine Corps.

The most notable of Harnett's sons who participated in World War II was Major General William C. Lee. The Dunn native was a visionary in the field of mobile warfare and was responsible for the creation of the parachute units in the U.S. Army. For his pioneering efforts in this branch, Lee is often referred to as the, "Father of the Airborne."

William Carey Lee was born in Dunn on March 12, 1895 to Eldredge and Erma Lee. He attended school in his hometown, then attended college at both Wake Forest and North Carolina State (NC State). At the latter he played football, baseball, and was a member of the ROTC. He graduated from NC State in time to participate in World War I, in which he served as a lieutenant. Following the war, Lee decided to make a career out of the army. He taught military science at NC State, served a tour in Panama, and graduated from Tank School.

In the years leading up to World War II, Lee was a vocal advocate of the establishment of a force of airborne soldiers in the U.S. Army. In June 1940, he was instrumental in the initial formation of a "test platoon" of parachutists. This eventually led to the creation in March of 1941 of the Provisional Parachute Group and the 501st Parachute Regiment. This in turn grew into the U.S.

This is a portrait of Major General William C. Lee, the "Father of the Airborne."

Airborne Command, created in March of 1942 and commanded by Lee, who was promoted to the rank of brigadier general on April 19, 1942. Lee's work led to the creation of two divisions of airborne troops, the 82nd Airborne and the 101st Airborne.

On August 10, 1942, he was promoted to major general and given command of the 101st Airborne Division. He worked tirelessly preparing his division for their future role in the liberation of Europe.

In the fall of 1943, General Lee devised the airborne tactics for an invasion of Normandy. He worked closely with generals such as Dwight Eisenhower and Omar Bradley in selecting drop zones and planning the airborne phase of Operation Overlord. A heart attack that Lee suffered on February 5, 1944 deprived him of the opportunity to accompany his men in the invasion. Unable to actively participate further in the war, General Lee was sent home in April of 1944 to recuperate.

General Lee was well liked by his men, many of whom were disappointed he would not be accompanying them in the upcoming battle. Lee's replacement, General Maxwell Taylor, urged his men to remember their stricken leader by replacing their normal cry of "Geronimo" with "Bill Lee" when they exited the planes. Thus, in the opening hours of the D-Day invasion, the name of Harnett native Bill Lee rang out across the French countryside.

Major General William C. Lee retired from the army in December 1944. He spent the final years of his life in Dunn, where he often entertained military leaders and other dignitaries. He died on March 1, 1948, and was buried in Greenwood cemetery. His house today serves as a museum.

9. THE MODERN ERA

With the end of World War II, Harnett began to change. In the 1940s, the landscape was dominated by farms and rural scenes, but by the end of the century, it was dominated by middle-class suburban houses and mobile homes. The number of individuals who made their living from small farms dwindled as most Harnett residents began looking outside the county for employment.

The 1950 Census showed that Harnett's population had grown to 47,605. In 1970, the population was 49,667, a modest increase over 20 years. But for the final decades of the twentieth century, Harnett's population would begin to explode, challenging the capability of officials to keep pace with such issues as urban sprawl and school overcrowding.

KOREAN WAR

In 1950, the United States was called upon to help prevent the fall of South Korea to the communists of North Korea. After initial difficulties, the combined American and United Nations forces were able to push the communists out of Korea and into China. The Chinese came to the aid of their Korean comrades, driving the American forces south once again. Eventually, the opposing forces held a position slightly north of the 38th parallel. By the time an armistice was signed on July 27, 1953, 36,516 Americans had given their lives to keep South Korea free.

Several Harnett Countians participated in the Korean War. At least 11 are known to have lost their lives in military action in Korea between 1950 and 1953.

CONSTRUCTION OF I-95

One of the most extensive and important transportation links in Harnett's history had its beginnings in 1956 when President Dwight Eisenhower signed the Federal-Aid Highway Act.

This authorized the creation of a network of limited access four-lane highways patterned after the German Autobahn system. Formally, it was called the Dwight D. Eisenhower System of Interstate and Defense Highways. Initial plans for the

President Harry Truman visits with the Dunn Knee Pants Baseball League in 1947.

system called for 41,000 miles of "Interstates" to be completed by 1975. The roads were to be built under the direction of the individual states, with 90 percent of the funds coming from the federal government.

The easternmost road in the network was designated as I-95 and linked the great cities of the eastern seaboard from Maine to Florida. One of the first portions of I-95 to be constructed and opened to the public was the section stretching from Kenly in Johnston County, across Harnett County to Eastover in Cumberland County. The route, which paralleled U.S. 301 through this area, was officially dedicated in February of 1960.

By the end of the twentieth century, I-95 stretched for 1,907 miles from Miami, Florida north to the Canadian border at Houlton, Maine. According to the North Carolina Department of Transportation, on average, 80,000 cars pass through Dunn on I-95 each day.

COURTHOUSE REMODELED

In January of 1959, county commissioners approved architectural plans for the second remodeling of the courthouse in the twentieth century. Efforts had been underway for some time to modernize the old courthouse or to erect a new one in Lillington.

Proponents of this project, though unsuccessful, were resilient. An article in the March 2, 1959 *Daily Record* notes, "Citizens of Harnett several times voted against a new courthouse, but the county board got around that legal technicality by having the legislature specify that delinquent tax collections be used for that purpose."

Frank Simpson was the architect chosen for the job, but his original plans were not followed as commissioners looked for ways to economize. There was not as much space in the finished structure as had been originally planned.

But the main drawbacks of the new courthouse, drawbacks that would play a key role in the public's future displeasure with the structure, were the lack of adequate public restroom facilities and the lack of an elevator so that the elderly and disabled could easily make their way to the second-floor courtrooms. These were not easy problems to fix.

Despite this, the county court held its first meeting in the remodeled courthouse on June 9, 1960.

When members of North Carolina State's School of Design visited the Harnett County Courthouse during an architectural survey of the state's courthouses in the 1970s, they were not impressed with what they found.

"The 1898 Harnett County Courthouse has been stripped of its unique Mission Style architectural details and lies encased in an undistinguished brick veneer shell created in 1959, then the building was enlarged and remodeled. . . . The interior has also been thoroughly institutionalized."

ERWIN, COMPANY TOWN
TO INCORPORATED MUNICIPALITY

In December of 1950, Erwin took the first steps in the process of growing beyond a mill town when Erwin Mills announced that it was selling the houses the company owned in the town.

Up to this point, virtually all the residents in Erwin rented their homes from Erwin Mills. On the morning of January 22, 1951, Erwin Mills sold 672 homes at prices ranging from $1,500 to $6,500.

The sale was conducted by Alester Furman Co. in the recreational building of the Methodist church. Only employees of the mill were eligible to participate in the sale.

Fifteen years later, residents took over the day-to-day operations of the town, which was officially incorporated as a municipality in 1967. According to the 1970 census, the population of the county's youngest municipality was 4,500.

This 1956 photograph shows the Harnett County Courthouse before remodeling. (Courtesy North Carolina Department of Archives and History.)

VIET NAM WAR

In the 1960s America became deeply involved in the fight against the spread of communism in southeast Asia. By the time the United States's involvement came to a close, 57,605 Americans had been killed in the Viet Nam War.

Figures for the number of individuals from Harnett County who died in the war vary. One source places the death toll at 20, while a statue on the grounds of the courthouse in Lillington lists 24. The first Harnett native to lose his life in the Viet Nam War was Staff Sergeant Donald D. Stewart of Coats, a member of the Air Force's 309th Commando Squadron. In December of 1965, a plane he was flying in crashed into a mountain near Tuy Hoa, Viet Nam.

During the conflict in Viet Nam, a ship named for Harnett County saw extensive action in the waters of southeast Asia. The U.S.S. *Harnett County* was built by the Missouri Valley Bridge and Iron Works in Evansville, Indiana in the fall of 1944. She was launched on October 27, 1944 and commissioned by the

Climbing the greasy pole was a popular event at Fourth of July celebrations like this one in Erwin c. 1960. (Courtesy Coastal Piedmont Leader.)

Navy on November 22, 1944 as the U.S.S. *LST-821*. The vessel was 528 feet long, 50 feet wide, displaced 1,625 tons, and had a draught of 11 feet. It was powered by two GM 12-567, V-12 diesel engines and was capable of speeds up to 12 knots. Her weaponry consisted of a dozen 20 millimeter anti-aircraft guns and eight 40 millimeter guns.

The U.S.S. *LST-821* saw limited action during World War II but did join the fray in time to take part in the attack on Okinawa in April of 1945. Her role was to transport supplies and men of the 77th Infantry Division. This was the ship's only taste of combat operations during the war.

Following the surrender of Japan, the ship returned to Vancouver, Washington. On July 8, 1946, she was decommissioned and placed in the Pacific Reserve Fleet. While a member of this fleet of inactive ships, the U.S.S. *LST-821* was officially renamed the U.S.S. *Harnett County* on July 1, 1955.

As the war in Viet Nam intensified and American involvement grew, the government found it necessary to bring several ships back into service. On August 20, 1966, the U.S.S. *Harnett County* was reactivated. The ship underwent repairs and modernization, the most noticeable change being the addition of a landing pad for helicopters.

In January of 1967 the U.S.S. *Harnett County* began operations with the river patrol forces operating in the Mekong River Delta in South Viet Nam. The ship spent its time transporting personnel, landing helicopters, providing fire support, and supporting smaller craft in the river campaign. On August 17, 1969, the ship earned the distinction of being the first of the LST class to log 5,000 accident-free helicopter landings.

The ship participated in several military operations during the war, including Operation Game Warden, Operation Giant Slingshot, Operation Searchturn, and Operation Breezy Cove. During the Tet Offensive in the winter of 1968, official reports note that the ship "utilized her full potential fire power in aggressive attacks upon Viet Cong strongholds and defending friendly units." Several times, the ship was attacked by saboteurs.

In August of 1970, the ship sailed to Guam, where her crew prepared her to be turned over to the Republic of Viet Nam. On October 12, 1970, the U.S.S. *Harnett County* was officially transferred to the Vietnamese Navy during ceremonies held on Guam. Her last captain was Lieutenant Commander F.M. Kirk Jr., who turned over the vessel to Lieutenant Commander Vu Nhan. The new owners changed the ship's name to the *My Tho* (HQ-800), and the vessel was used in operations for the South Vietnamese Navy until the spring of 1975. The ship was purchased on April 5, 1976 by the Republic of the Philippines and is presumed to still be in service to that country as the transport ship *Sierra Madre* (LT 57).

In her service as an American warship, the U.S.S. *Harnett County* received several commendations. The ship received one battle star during World War II and, during the Viet Nam War, received nine battle stars, two Presidential Unit Citations, and three Navy Unit Commendations.

This official U.S. Navy photo taken in 1969 shows two river patrol boats leaving the U.S.S. Harnett County for a patrol along the Co Chein River in the Mekong Delta.

FOUNDING OF RAVEN ROCK STATE PARK

During the mid-twentieth century, developers and loggers became interested in acquiring the land along the remote reaches of the Cape Fear River near Raven Rock.

In the 1960s, Dr. Robert Soots of Campbell College led an effort to preserve the natural beauty of the area for the enjoyment and education of future generations. State Senator William W. Staton introduced a bill in the General Assembly on April 18, 1969 that created a state park along the river surrounding the rock.

143

This was the first state park created since Mount Mitchell State Park back in 1915.

On March 23, 1970, the state purchased the first tract of land for the park, the J.C. Cummings tract consisting of 221.7 acres. Shortly thereafter, Burlington Industries donated 169.4 acres for the park.

By the beginning of the twenty-first century, the park contained 3,549 acres of land. Raven Rock State Park has been a boon to the Harnett economy, thanks to the large numbers of visitors who flock to the county to enjoy the facility. In the year 2000, the park hosted 111,695 visitors.

This is a photograph of Wade Lucas of Erwin, at right, prominent newspaper reporter and writer. (Courtesy Sion Harrington III.)

This aerial photo shows Erwin c. 1970.

SCHOOL CONSOLIDATION

As early as 1963, proponents were working for centralizing the local community schools into a system of consolidated high schools. The proposal was not a popular one with most Harnett citizens, who voted down bond referendums in 1963, 1967, 1973, and 1974.

Undeterred by the will of the populace, county commissioners voted for an ad velorem tax increase in 1974 to pay for construction of three new high schools.

The first two of these consolidated schools were Western Harnett High School and Harnett Central High School, both officially dedicated in May of 1978.

The final school, serving the people of eastern Harnett, was dedicated in November of 1986. This school was called Triton, in honor of the three towns from which it draws its pupils.

145

HARNETT POLITICIANS MAKE MARK ON STATE AND NATIONAL AFFAIRS

The second half of the twentieth century witnessed the rise of several Harnett residents to high elective office within both state and federal government. During the final three decades of the century, someone from Harnett County held an office on the North Carolina Council of State as well as in the U.S. Congress, a feat rarely matched by other counties of like size.

The trailblazer of these politicians was Robert Morgan of Lillington. Morgan attained his first political office at the age of 25 when he was elected Harnett clerk of court in 1950. He had the distinction of being the youngest clerk of court in North Carolina. In 1954 Morgan was elected to the North Carolina Senate from the 15th District. He was named president pro tempore of that body in 1965. Among his many achievements in the state senate was the establishment of a medical school at East Carolina University.

The railroad depot was a prominent landmark in Dunn.

146

This is an early photograph of the smokestack at Erwin Mills.

Morgan became the first Harnett native to be elected to a seat on the North Carolina Council of State when he was elected attorney general in 1968. A successful and popular attorney general, he was re-elected in 1972. His achievements earned him the Wyman Award, given by the attorneys general from across the United States to the most outstanding attorney general in the country. But the pinnacle of Morgan's political career was reached in 1974 when he was elected to serve in the United States Senate. Senator Morgan is the only Harnett resident to ever serve in the U.S. Senate.

Bob Etheridge began his political career on the Harnett County Board of Commissioners, serving from 1973 to 1977. Upon the urgings of many friends, Etheridge ran for and won a seat in the North Carolina House of Representatives, representing the 19th House District for five terms.

In 1988, Etheridge was elected North Carolina Superintendent of Public Instruction, becoming the second Harnett resident to serve on the North Carolina Council of State. He served two terms in that office and, in 1996, ran successfully for the U.S. Congress. He continues to represent the people of the 2nd Congressional District in the U.S. Congress as the twenty-first century begins.

In 1994, Campbell University professor and former ambassador to Romania Dr. David Funderburk made his mark on Harnett politics by being elected to the U.S. Congress from the 2nd Congressional District. His election was significant for two reasons.

He was the first Harnett resident to serve in the U.S. House of Representatives since Hannibal Godwin left office nearly 70 years earlier. Of more significance, however, is the fact that he is the only Republican from Harnett to be elected to anything other than a local office or the General Assembly. Funderburk was instrumental in bringing Republican presidential candidate Pat Buchanan to Campbell University in 1996, the latter being the first presidential candidate to campaign in Harnett County. (Herbert Hoover made a campaign stop in Dunn in October of 1927, but he had not officially declared himself a candidate for the 1928 election.)

The most remarkable female politician from Harnett is, without argument, Elaine Marshall, who was elected to the North Carolina Senate to represent the 15th District in 1992. Two years later, following a bizarre election recount that ended in a tie, she lost her seat in a run-off election to Dan Page of Coats. Not to be disheartened by this setback, Marshall won the Democratic Party's nomination for secretary of state in 1996. Facing what many believed to be an impossible task, Marshall campaigned vigorously against the Republican nominee, race car driving legend Richard Petty. Marshall's hard work and perseverance paid off, and she defeated Petty in the November 1996 elections. Thus, she became the first woman ever elected to an office on the North Carolina Council of State. Secretary of State Marshall was re-elected in 2000.

It should be noted that Harnett is also home to a prominent jurist. Judge Stanley Gerald Arnold began his political career in Harnett County with his election to the General Assembly in 1970. In 1974, he was elected to fill the unexpired term of Judge William E. Graham on the North Carolina Court of Appeals. He served as chief judge of the North Carolina Court of Appeals during the late 1990s.

THE MILL IN ERWIN CLOSES

Passage of the North American Free Trade Agreement (NAFTA) in 1994 was a lethal blow to the thriving textile industry in the South. Unable to compete with the cheap labor and lax environmental regulations of Third World countries, many American industrialists either closed their factories outright or shifted their operations to Mexico.

Erwin Mills was not immune to this trend. What was once touted as the largest denim factory in the world faced many cutbacks in the mid-1990s. Unable to

Cameron Hill Presbyterian Church in Johnsonville has been a prominent landmark in western Harnett since the 1890s.

This shoulder patch was worn by some of the sailors who served aboard the U.S.S. Harnett County *in the Viet Nam War.*

compete with the companies utilizing virtual slave labor, the mill ceased operation in 2000. Not only did the county loose its largest civilian employer, Harnett lost one of its major taxpayers. But the company that had begun as a sideline for the prosperous Duke family had made an important and lasting contribution to the county, providing jobs for thousands of people for most of the twentieth century.

HARNETT IN THE 2000 CENSUS

Data from the 2000 Census demonstrated that the county has changed dramatically since it came into being 145 years earlier. The county claimed 91,025 inhabitants, making it the 27th largest county in the state. The population had grown by 34.2 percent in the decade of the 1990s. This dramatic growth was mainly due to two factors—urban sprawl from Raleigh to the north, and the growth of Fort Bragg to the south. The inhabitants of Harnett could boast of a median household income of $31,941.

CONCLUSION

As has been demonstrated, Harnett has seen many changes over the past 150 years. Born on the eve of war, the county struggled under severe economic disadvantages for half a century but prospered throughout the twentieth century. As the twentieth century draws to an end and the twenty-first begins, it is appropriate to take a look back at our county and see how the Harnett of today differs from the Harnett of the nineteenth century.

Contemplate things today, at the dawn of the twenty-first century, that modern residents of Harnett County take for granted. People travel to places like Raleigh and Fayetteville in a matter of minutes, communicate with people all over the world in an instant, eat fresh foods year round that are grown all over the world, wear clothes made predominately in southeast Asia, and are less than 24-hours travel time away from the remotest parts of the globe. We have watched live television broadcasts from the moon and Mars, and, via the internet, we can download photos from the remote reaches of space.

These would have been wondrous events for our ancestors 150 years ago. To have predicted such things would one day be commonplace would have led one to be branded as either a dreamer or a lunatic! The trip to Raleigh and Fayetteville was under the best of circumstances a two- or three-day round trip with mule and wagon. Most communications with the outside world were via the U.S. mail, and most clothes were made at home. With only a few exceptions, food was grown on an individual's farm or produced by a local farmer, and preserved for use through the winter. It took days or weeks to reach some parts of the globe, and there were still some regions of the world where civilized men had not tread. As for visiting the heavenly bodies, such dreams were left to science fiction writers, as mankind had not yet even taken flight.

One can only imagine the changes that will be wrought on the Harnett landscape as another century and a half passes.

Erwin Overall Days was the predecessor of Denim Days. In its heyday, Erwin produced more denim than any other factory in the world.

BIBLIOGRAPHY

Adams, Agatha. *Paul Green of Chapel Hill*. Chapel Hill, NC: University of North Carolina Library, 1951.

Adams, Joel, et. al. *Voices of Yesteryear*. 1969.

Ashe, Samuel A. *History of North Carolina*. 2 volumes. Greensboro, NC: C.L. Van Noppen, 1925.

Autry, Jerry. *General William C. Lee Father of the Airborne*. 1995.

Bradley, Stephen. *North Carolina Confederate Militia Officers Roster*. Wilmington, NC: Broadfoot Publishing Company, 1992.

Burns, Robert, ed. *100 Courthouses A Report on North Carolina Judicial Facilities*. 2 volumes. 1978.

Clark, Victor. *Colorful Heritage Documented*. 1989.

Clark, Walter, ed. *Histories of the Several Regiments and Battalions from North Carolina*. 5 volumes. Raleigh, NC: State of North Carolina, 1905.

——. *The State Records of North Carolina*. 15 volumes. 1895–1903.

Comer, James Vann. *Descendants of Colonel Archibald McDugald, Sr., and Rebecca Buie*. 1991.

Foote, William Henry. *Sketches of North Carolina*. New York: R. Carter, 1846.

Fowler, Malcolm. *They Passed This Way*. Harnett County Centennial, 1955.

——. *Valley of the Scots*. W. Fowle, 1986.

Fraser, Alexander. *United Empire Loyalists*. 2 volumes. Baltimore, MD: Genealogical Publishing Company, 1904.

Green, Herman. *A History of Dunn*. Dunn, NC: H.P. Green, 1985.

Green, Paul. *Highland Call*. Chapel Hill, NC: University of North Carolina Press, 1941.

——. *Paul Green's Wordbook*. 2 volumes. Chapel Hill, NC: University of North Carolina Press, 1990.

Grill, C. Franklin. *Methodism in the Upper Cape Fear*. 1966.

Harrington, Sion, and John Hairr. *Eyewitnesses to Averasboro*. 2001.

Hasty, Mary Alice, et. al., eds. *Heritage of Harnett County*. Erwin, NC: The Heritage of Harnett Book Committee, 1993.

Hoffman, Glenn. *A History of the Atlantic Coast Line Railroad Company*. CSX Corporate Communications and Public Affairs, 1998.

Johnson, Guion Griffis. *Antebellum North Carolina*. Chapel Hill, NC: University of North Carolina Press, 1937.

Jordan, Weymouth and Louis Manarin, eds. *North Carolina Troops 1861–1865 A Roster*. 19 volumes. Raleigh, NC: State Department of Archives and History, 1966–1998.

Journey, Robert. *Soil Survey of Harnett County, North Carolina*. 1916.

Kivett, Everett McNeill. *The McNeill's Ferry Chronicle*. Burnsville, NC: Yancey Graphics, 1983.

Lefler, Hugh, and Alfred Ray Newsome. *North Carolina: The History of a Southern State*. Chapel Hill, NC: University of North Carolina Press, 1954.

MacKenzie, James. *Colorful Heritage*. 1969.

McLean, J.P. *An Historical Account of the Settlement of Scottish Highlanders in America*. 1900.

——. *Flora MacDonald in America*. Lumberton, NC: A.W. McLean, 1909.

Meyer, Duane. *The Highland Scots of North Carolina*. Raleigh, NC: Carolina Charter Tercentenary Commission, 1963.

Moore, John W. *Roster of North Carolina Troops in the War Between the States*. 4 volumes. Raleigh, NC: Ash & Gatling, 1882.

This 1908 postcard of the second bridge at Duke carries the inscription, "Second highest bridge in America, Duke N.C." (Courtesy Erwin Historical Society.)

This is an early view of the Hotel Lillington.

Oates, John. *The Story of Fayetteville*. Charlotte, NC: The Dowd Press, 1950.

Page, Hubbard Fulton. *Lyrics and Legends of the Cape Fear Country*. Durham, NC: Presses of Christian Printing Company, 1932.

Pearce, J. Winston. *Campbell College: Big Miracle at Little Buies Creek*. Nashville, TN: Broadman Press, 1976.

Powell, Joey, and John Hairr. *Ghost Towns on the Upper Cape Fear*. Erwin, NC: Averasboro Press, 1996.

Powell, William, ed. *Dictionary of North Carolina Biography*. 5 volumes. Chapel Hill, NC: University of North Carolina Press, 1979–1996.

——. *North Carolina Gazetteer*. Chapel Hill, NC: University of North Carolina Press, 1968.

——. *North Carolina Through Four Centuries*. Chapel Hill, NC: University of North Carolina Press, 1989.

Rock, Collie. *Neill Shaw Stewart, Esq.: A Biographical Study*. Erwin, NC: C.E. Rock, 1983.

Ross, Malcolm. *The Cape Fear*. New York: Holt, Rinehart and Winston, 1965.

Russel, Phillips. *North Carolina in the Revolutionary War*. Charlotte, NC: Heritage Printers, 1965.

Saunders, William L. *The Colonial Records of North Carolina.* 10 volumes. Raleigh, NC: P.M. Hale State Printer, 1886–1890.

Sharp, Bill. *A New Geography of North Carolina.* 4 volumes. Raleigh, NC: Sharpe Publishing Company, 1954–1965.

Sitterson, Joseph. *The Secession Movement in North Carolina.* Chapel Hill, NC: University of North Carolina Press, 1939.

Spangler, Daniel. *Soil Survey of Harnett County, North Carolina.* 1995.

Troxler, Carole Waterson. *The Loyalist Experience in North Carolina.* Raleigh, NC: North Carolina Department of Cultural Resources, Division of Archives and History, 1976.

Wheeler, John H. *Historical Sketches of North Carolina.* Philadelphia, PA: Lippincott, Grambo and Company, 1851.

Wicker, Rassie. *Miscellaneous Ancient Records of Moore County.* Southern Pines, NC: Moore County Historical Association, 1971.

Dunn High School operated from 1907 to 1926.

INDEX

Anderson Creek, 14, 27, 31, 67, 124, 130

Angier, 9, 12, 94, 99, 100, 115, 124

Angier, Jonathan Cicero, 99–100

Argyll Colony, 20–22

Atlantic & Western Railroad, 107

Avera, Alexander, 35

Averasboro, 20, 35, 38, 45, 46, 49, 60, 73, 74, 75, 80, 81, 83, 86, 94

Averasboro, battle of, 64–65, 69

Barbecue Presbyterian Church, 26–27, 30, 32

Black River, 11, 12, 18, 20, 23, 64, 69, 80

Boone Trail, 121, 124

Buckhorn Falls, 36, 37, 67, 78

Buckhorn Hills, 16, 46, 67

Buckhorn Iron Works, 15, 46, 66–67, 71, 78

Buie's Creek, 94, 97, 99, 115, 120, 124, 128

Buie's Creek Academy, 97

Bunnlevel, 104, 122, 130

Cameron's Hill, 10, 15, 27, 33, 43, 126

Cameron Hill Fire Tower, 126

Campbell College, 97, 143, 148

Campbell, James A., 97

Campbell, Reverend James, 27, 97

Cape Fear & Northern Railroad, 99–100

Cape Fear River, 9, 12, 14–15, 18–20, 22–24, 26–28, 31–32, 35–38, 40, 44–46, 52, 58, 60, 64, 66, 69, 71, 75, 78, 83–84, 93–94, 96, 100–101, 103, 109, 122, 128, 130, 143

Chalybeate Springs, 15, 49, 63, 104, 122, 130

Coats, 9, 94, 100, 122–124, 140, 148

Coffield, C.H., 49–52, 63, 77

Cornwallis, Lord, 32–33

Court of Pleas and Quarter Sessions, 24, 55–56

Courthouse, 24, 54, 57, 59–60, 64, 75, 81–83, 85–90, 97, 109–110, 124, 139–140

Cumberland Academy, 54–55, 57

Cumberland County, 9, 12, 16, 22–24, 28, 31, 33, 35, 37, 40, 43–45, 49, 51, 53–54, 57, 59, 69, 75, 80, 109, 126, 130, 138

Denim, 101–102, 125, 149

Duke family, 100, 102, 126, 150

Duncan, 108–109

Dunn, 9, 11–12, 79–86, 88–89, 93–94, 99, 109–110, 120–121, 124, 130–133, 135, 138, 148

Eden Colony, 106

Erwin/Erwin Mills, 9, 12, 14, 22, 31, 36, 71, 102, 120–121, 124, 126, 139, 149, 100–102, 139, 149

Etheridge, Bob, 148

Fanning, Colonel David, 33

Fayetteville & Western Plank Road, 10, 40–45

Ferries, 24, 28, 44–45, 75, 83, 86, 94

Fish Creek, 9

Flatwoods, 9–10

Folsome's Tavern, 31

Fort Bragg, 9, 117–118, 122, 126, 133, 150

Fowler, Malcolm, 17–18, 30, 56, 59, 67, 74, 77

Godwin, Hannibal, 93–94, 110, 148

Green, Paul, 128

Green, Sheriff John A., 53, 75, 77, 85, 89

Green's Path, 18–19, 24

Hector's Creek, 9

Native Americans, 16, 18, 19, 22, 26, 40, 140

Interstate 95, 137–138

Johnson, Sam, 41, 53

Johnson, Sheriff James, 53, 56

Johnsonville, 10, 15, 41, 54, 86, 124

Kipling, 104, 115, 122

Ku Klux Klan, 73

Lee, General William C., 133–135

Lillington, 9–10, 12, 15, 31, 38, 59–60, 64, 71, 75, 80–83, 85–87, 89–91, 94, 96–97, 103–104, 106–111, 120–122, 124, 130, 139–140

Lillington Bridge, 94, 96, 128–130

Linden, 10, 12, 31, 44, 104

Lower Little River, 12, 19, 24, 31–32, 51, 54, 96, 109

Luart, 107

MacDonald, Flora, 15, 27, 28

McCormick, John, 75, 78, 82

McDugald, Archibald, 33

McKay, John, 44, 53–54, 57

McLeod, Sergeant Stanley, 132–133

McNeill, John, 57, 59

McNeill, Sheriff Kenneth, 77

Mamers, 10, 15, 107, 120

Marshall, Elaine, 148

Mingo Swamp, 9, 12, 18, 28, 109

Mining, 15–16, 46, 67, 78

Morgan, Robert, 146, 148

Mounds, Native American, 16–18

Olive, Will, 113

Olivia, 10, 47, 113

Overhills, 118–120

Pee Dee River, 18–19, 24, 40

Pegram, George W., 51, 53, 56

Piedmont, 9, 14, 43–44, 104

Pineview, 10, 46–47, 104, 126

Plank Road, 10, 40, 44–45

Purvis, Ed, 88

This parade in Lillington was part of the 1955 Harnett Centennial celebrations.

This photograph of a circus day in Dunn was taken October 14, 1902.

Raleigh & Cape Fear Railroad, 102–104

Raleigh–Fayetteville Stage Road, 38, 40

Raven Rock State Park, 67, 130, 143–144

Ross, Neill, 128, 130

Route 60, 120–121

Route 301, 120, 138

Sandhills, 9, 10, 12, 16, 20, 24, 30, 40, 47, 106, 111, 113, 117

Seminole, 107, 120

Shaw, Dushee, 22, 40, 71

Sherman, General William T., 64, 67, 69, 71

Smiley's Falls, 14, 24, 36–38, 100–101

South Black River, 12

Spout Springs, 10, 15, 47, 68, 71, 104

Springs, 12, 14–15, 27–28, 104, 130

Stewart, Alton, 122–124

Summerville, 15, 44, 46, 54–57, 63–64, 71, 87

Toomer, 44, 51, 53, 57–60

Turlington's Crossroads, 86

Tuscarora War, 19

Upper Little River, 12, 15, 17, 32–33, 60, 86, 106, 130

U.S.S. *Harnett County*, 140, 142

Western Railroad, 46–47, 66, 68, 118

Williams, Dr. John Taylor, 91

Wilson Short Cut Railroad, 80

These Erwin Mill officials are shown crossing the Duke Bridge shortly after it opened in 1904. In the first buggy is James B. Duke, the second carries F.L. Fuller and Benjamin Duke, and the third contains W.A. Erwin and T.J. Walker. (Courtesy North Carolina Department of Archives and History.)